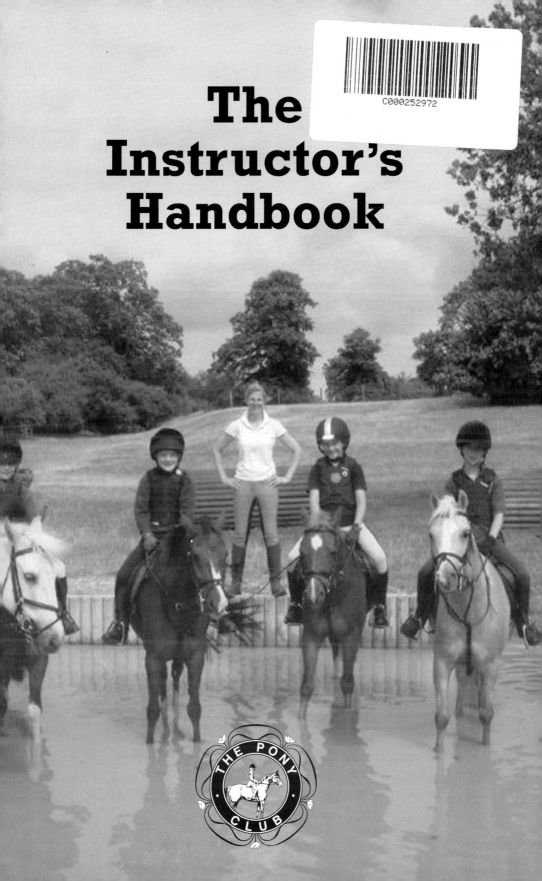

The Instructor's Handbook

C000252972

The Pony Club
Stoneleigh Park
Kenilworth
Warwickshire
CV8 2RW

Website: www.pcuk.org

Published in the UK by The Pony Club

© 2010 The Pony Club

First published 1955
First paperback edition (updated) 1993
Reprinted 1996, 2000
Reprinted with new illustrations 2005

British Library Cataloguing-in-Publication Data
A catalogue record for this book
is available from the British Library

ISBN 978-1-907279-06-5

Designed by Alan Hamp
Diagrams by Victor Shreeve
Illustrations by Maggie Raynor
Printed in Great Britain by Halstan & Co.

Trade disribution by Kenilworth Press
An Imprint of Quiller Publishing Ltd
Wykey House, Wykey, Shrewsbury, SY4 1JA
Tel: 01939 261616 Fax: 01939 261606
E-mail: info@quillerbooks.com
Website: www.kenilworthpress.co.uk

Contents

Preface   7

The Basics of Pony Club Instruction 9

1. **General Principles 10**
    Qualities of a Good Coach/Instructor 10
    Preparation Before the Rally 10
    Health and Safety 11
        Risk Assessment 11
        Visual Assessment 11
    Principles of Good Riding Instruction 12
    First Aid 12
    Whether to Instruct Mounted or Dismounted 13

2. **Various Activities and Forms of Instruction 14**
    Forms of Instruction–Mounted 15
        Class Lesson 15
        Instructional Hack or Country Ride 16
        Formation Riding 17
        Mock Hunt 17
        Paper Chase 18
        Scavenger Hunt 18
        Gymkhana Games 19
        Dressage Lesson 19
        Show-Jumping Lesson 19
        Cross-Country Lessons 20
        Road Safety Lesson 20
        Discussion 20
    Forms of Instruction–Dismounted 21
        Practical Horse and Pony Care 21
        Stable Management Tasks 21
        Textbook Instruction in *The Manual of Horsemanship* 22
        Video or DVD 22
        Quiz 23
        Lecture 23
        Discussion 23

3. **Use of the Voice 24**
    How to Breathe Correctly 24

Taking the Mounted Ride 25

4. **Controlling the Ride During a Class Lesson 26**
    The Riding Area 26
    Order of Riding 28
    Directive Terms 28
    Position of the Coach/Instructor 28
    Words of Command 29
        The Three Functions–Examples 29
        Commanding School Movements 29
        Sample Turns and Changes of Rein 30
        To Halt and Move Off 32
    School Manners and Discipline 33

5. **Procedure for Giving a Class Lesson 34**
    Introduction and Inspection 35
        The Riding Area 36
        Organising the Ride 36
    Assessing and Working-In the Ride 36

5. Procedure for Giving a Class Lesson *(continued)*
Basic Corrections 36
Physical Exercises 37
The Lesson of the Day 37
Period of Relaxation 38
Jumping 38
Games 38
Ending the Lesson / Warm Down 39
Reflection / Self-Evaluation 39

6. Instructing Beginners and the Very Young 39
Extra Items Which Will Be Required 39
Extra Saddlery to Be Checked 40
Special Considerations When Taking the Ride 40
Sample Lessons 41
    Moving Off and Stopping 41
    Turns and Circles 41
    Rising Trot 43
    Transition to Canter 43

7. Developing the Rider's Position 45
Teaching the Correct Position 45

8. Physical Exercises 48
A Few Exercises Used for Specific Purposes 48
Checks to be Made During Exercises 50

Jumping 51

9. Instruction in Jumping 52
The Aims of the Coach/Instructor 52
The Position of the Ride and the Coach/Instructor 52
Island Fences 53
Fence Alongside a Hedge 53
A Junior Ride 54
A Large, More Competent Ride 55
Planning the Jumping Lesson 55
Taking the Jumping Lesson 56
Teaching Riders to Jump 57
Encouraging Ponies to Jump Well 58

10. The Rider's Position When Jumping 59
Developing the Rider's Position When Jumping 59
Common Problems in the Approach 60
Common Problems During the Jump 63
Common Problems on Landing 65
Other Common Problems 66
    Lack of Confidence 66
    Pain 66

11. Jumping Exercises Needing a Small Amount of Equipment 66
1. Jumping from a Trot 66
2. Jumping off a Circle 67
3. Doubles 67
4. Cross-Poles 68
5. Counting Strides 69
6. Gradients 69
7. Ditches 70
8. Jumping from Different Angles 70
9. Jumping from Slow and Fast Speeds 71

Taking the Dismounted Ride 73

12. Instruction in Horse and Pony Care 74
The Dismounted Group Lesson 74
    Preparation 74
Grooming 74
    Before the Lesson 75
    Taking the Lesson 75

Other Subjects (Using Lesson Plan for Grooming) 75
Shoeing 76
    To be Taught Before 'B' Test 76
    Preliminary Lessons 76
    Follow-Up Lessons 77
    Practical Demonstration 77
The Five-Minute Talk 78
Horse Care Tasks 78

13. Giving a Lecture 78
Points to Remember 79

14. Using Audio Visual Equipment 80
Requirements 80
Suggested Uses 80
The Video Camera 81
Warnings 81
Suggestions for Filming:
    1. A Jumping Lesson 81
    2. A Movement to Ride 82
    3. Horse and Pony Care 82
    4. Other Suggestions 82

Further Subjects for Instruction 83

15. Countryside Studies and Hunting 84
Ways of Teaching Countryside Studies 84
Hunting 85
    Ways of Teaching Hunting 85

16. Road Safety 86
Early Training 86
The Object of the Tests 86
Planning Instruction for the Tests:
    Mounted 86
    Dismounted (Indoors) 87

17. Preparing a Ride for Pony Club Competitions 87
(a) Riding a Dressage Test 87
    Before the Mounted Lesson:
        Learning the Test 88
        Checking the Rules 88
    The Mounted Lesson:
        Requirements 88
        Starting the Lesson 89
        Individual Practice in the Arena 89
    Conclusion 90
(b) Show Jumping 91
    The Course 91
    Assistants 91
    Walking the Course 91
    Preliminary Work on the Flat 92
    Jumping the Course in Sections 93
    Jumping the Whole Course 93
    The Second Round 93
    The Timed Jump-Off 94
(c) Riding Across Country 94
    General Considerations 94
    Speed Control 95
    The Course 95
    Fences with Obscure Landings 96
    Ditches 97
    Jumping into Water 97
    Corner Fences 97
    Tantivies 98
    Determination 98
    Conditioning and Fitness 98
    Cooling Off / Warming Down 98

For the More Experienced Coach/Instructor 99

18. School Movements Performed in Various Ways: Formation Riding 100
Numbering 100
Proving 100
Dividing into 'Rides' 100
Double Ride 101
Dressing 101
Arena or School 101
Working by Rides 101
Turning by Rides 102
Double Ride Work 102
A Drill Ride 102
Inclining Across the School 103
Four Ways of Performing Small Circles 103
Points to Remember 105
Tricycling 105
   Points to Remember 106
Producing a Formation Ride 108

19. The Difference Between an Instructor and a Coach 108
Assessing the Ride 109
Explanation and Demonstration 110
Practise 110
Feedback 110
Self-Evaluation 111

20. Improving Communication 111

21. A Riding Lesson or Traffic Direction? 112

22. Four Rides within a Ride 113

23. The Scale of Training 114

24. Smart Targets 116

25. Trotting-Poles and Gymnastic Jumping Exercises 116
Trotting-Poles 117
   Equipment 118
   Positioning of Equipment 118
   Method 118
   Trotting-Poles with One Jump 119
   Trotting-Poles with Two or Three Jumps 119
   Physical Exercises for Riders While Jumping 120
   Trotting-Poles with Fences at Bounce Distances 120
Gymnastics without Trotting-Poles 121
   Equipment 121
   Positioning of Equipment 121
   Method 121
Jumping Lanes 122
Warnings 122

26. Gaining More from a Session 123

27. Working a Rider on the Lunge 124
   Purpose 124
   Standard 124
   Requirements 125
   Method 125
   Exercises 126
   The More Advanced Rider 127

Appendix 128

Pony Club Standards of Efficiency 128
Polework and Jumping Distances 164

Index 165

Preface

This book is designed primarily to encourage those who lack experience in how to teach, and to refresh the memories of those who do not teach on a regular basis. It should be used in conjunction with the Pony Club's official textbooks: *The Manual of Horsemanship*, *Keeping a Pony at Grass*, and *Breeding, Backing and Bringing On Young Horses and Ponies*. *The Instructor's Folder*, containing The Pony Club Standards of Efficiency, is another useful guide.

Learning from a book can never be a substitute for attending Coaches'/Instructors' Courses and for experience gained while taking a ride, but these pages are intended to help Coaches/Instructors to clarify their ideas and to teach with confidence, developing their own style within the suggested guidelines.

We hope that the book will be inspiring and helpful to everyone who coaches/instructs for the Pony Club.

The Basics of Pony Club Instruction

1   General Principles

Working rallies are the backbone of the Pony Club. If they are enjoyable, young people will come to them and will benefit from what they are able to learn. The success of working rallies, therefore, depends on our Coaches/Instructors.

No one can be forced to learn; there must be a desire to do so. Young people will only learn if there is an incentive, if the lesson is presented in an interesting way and if they can understand the reason for what they are doing.

The Qualities of a Good Coach/Instructor
- Genuine liking for young people, horses and ponies, and a desire to help them.
- An alert and enthusiastic personality.
- Self-confidence, which gives the ride a feeling of security.
- Powers of observation which, when developed, will quickly spot and correct basic faults.
- A clear, carrying voice which is easy to listen to.

Potential Coaches/Instructors develop their ability by:
- Gaining a thorough knowledge of Pony Club methods as outlined in *The Manual of Horsemanship*.
- Studying the methods of more experienced Coaches/Instructors.
- Attending Coaches'/Instructors' courses.
- Plenty of practice, combined with self-analysis.

Preparation Before the Rally
The success of any lesson depends largely on how well it has been prepared.
- It is important to know how many will be in the ride, their ages, and their ability. You should also be aware of the facilities and the amount of time available.
- The Chief Coach/Instructor should tell you which stage the ride has reached in the Pony Club syllabus. This will help you to decide what should be taught next.
- Work out the object of your lesson; know what you are aiming to achieve.
- Make an outline plan, such as:
  1. Introduction, tack check, ask about pony and rider combination
  2. Assessment and work in
  3. Revision
  4. Explanation and demonstration of new subject to be taught (or 'lesson of the day')
  5. Practice and corrections

6. Games
7. Warm down
8. Feedback and homework

- Prepare the 'lesson of the day' thoroughly, producing points in a logical order, which will make them easier to understand and to remember.
- Study the syllabus. Read the text book. Know your subject matter thoroughly, so that you can explain it clearly.
- Try to develop your own way of making the lesson memorable and enjoyable.
- Prepare notes if it will help you, but do not read your lesson out, as this would be dull for your ride.
- Decide what props you will need, depending on your lesson plan and which games you will use.
- Decide whether you will need an assistant and/or a horse. Make the necessary arrangements.
- When teaching with video or DVDs, make sure that either you or your assistant are familiar with the equipment and are able to use it correctly.
- Be prepared to adapt your lesson; circumstances can change in the best administrations.
- Teach a little, well.
- Plan to keep your ride SAFE, HAPPY AND ALERT.

Health and Safety
Safety is an essential factor when planning your lesson. Having worked out your plan you need to decide how to conduct the lesson safely.

Risk Assessment
The organiser will provide a written assessment of the significant risks for the rally. You need to consider the risks that are specific to your lesson, and bring to the attention of the organiser any risk that you think is significant (i.e. more than in normal riding) and the way in which you intend to control that risk.

Risk Assessment Guidelines and Check Lists for Pony Club Rallies and competitive disciplines are available from Headquarters.

Visual Assessment
When you arrive at the rally site, check carefully to see if there are any significant risks. If you have any concerns, discuss them with the rally organiser.

Principles of Good Riding Instruction

- Be well turned out. You and your horse (if you are mounted) should be an example to your ride.
- Arrive early. Have enough time to adapt to last-minute changes. Check the area allocated to you. Organise props, and brief your assistant.
- Establish a rapport with every member of the ride.
- Keep up the interest of the ride; keep them active and alert. AVOID TOO MUCH TALKING.
- Speak clearly. Be simple and definite.
- Be quick to observe the basic faults, and be understanding in correcting them.
- Praise even the slightest improvement.
- Ask questions of your ride on the work they are doing and encourage feedback: this helps riders to take ownership of their own learning.
- Have an enquiring, open mind. Try to find out why a rider, horse, or pony is experiencing a particular difficulty.
- Keep order but do not bully. Never be sarcastic.
- Be firm but sympathetic, especially with nervous riders.
- Keep your eyes on the whole ride.
- Avoid spending too much time with one individual; the others will become bored. Try to give all riders an equal amount of attention.
- Use the affirmative *'Do'* rather than *'Don't'*: e.g., *'Carry your hands higher'*, not *'Don't carry your hands so low!'*
- When making an individual correction, say the name before the correction, e.g., *'Jane... look up'*.
- When asking questions, say the name last, e.g., *'What is a skewbald horse... Mary?'* This makes the whole ride think of the answer.
- Confirm by practical tests and questions that your ride has mastered each stage of the lesson.
- Try to find the reason for any disruptive behaviour, and act accordingly.
- Never be destructive. After criticism be sure to rebuild confidence.
- Be cheerful and encouraging, ready to laugh at silly mishaps. Try to create in your ride the will to persevere.
- Know when to stop the working part of the lesson. Always end on a satisfactory note.

First Aid

It is recommended that all Coaches/Instructors should know the current BHS First Aid procedure. Ideally, they should hold the EFAW or ESFAC Trained First Aider Qualification. The rally organiser should tell you (a) what to do if you have an incident during your ride, and (b) who is the

First Aider and how to contact him or her. Make absolutely sure that you are given this information. Carry your mobile phone.

In the event of an accident, halt the ride immediately, keep calm, and use your common sense. If necessary, summon help. Once first aid has been applied, and if circumstances permit, reassure your ride and continue the lesson.

Members who, in the opinion of the Coach/Instructor, have been or might have been concussed, must not ride again on the same day.

All accidents must be reported to the organiser, who may ask you to make an entry in the Accident Book and to complete a Pony Club accident form.

Whether to Instruct Mounted or Dismounted

Instructing dismounted is more sensible when teaching junior rides. It is safer, and the closer human contact gives the riders more confidence. Demonstrate by one of the following methods:
1. Use the most competent member of the ride.
2. Use a mounted assistant, perhaps a Junior Coach/Instructor.
3. Give a mini-demonstration yourself, on foot.
4. Ride a suitable pony borrowed out of the ride.
Demonstrations should be as polished and correct as possible unless they are being used deliberately to show faults.

Instructing while mounted is essential when taking the ride out on hacks. It is often preferable with more competent rides because:
1. You can give your own demonstrations and can illustrate faults.
2. If your horse is suitable, you might let certain members ride him in order to feel his movement.
3. You will have more scope in controlling your ride:
   a) When giving a cross-country lesson.
   b) When working the ride in a large area.
   c) While moving the ride from one place to another.

Before teaching while mounted consider the following:
1. Is the ride likely to be under reasonable control?
2. Is your position good enough to be a worthy example to your ride? Members copy their Coach/Instructor, but are quick to note their faults.
3. Will your horse stand patiently for long periods so that you can devote your whole attention to the ride?
4. If the area is enclosed will it be large enough to accommodate the ride as well as a mounted Coach/Instructor?

2   Various Activities and Forms of Instruction

The responsibility for a branch's overall plan of progression should stem from the branch Chief Coach/Instructor. (He may or may not also be the District Commissioner.) Suggestions for planning camps, day rallies and shorter afternoon or evening rallies are covered in *The District Commissioner's Handbook*.

Rallies are sometimes delegated to Rally Organisers who work in conjunction with the Chief Instructor.

At a rally, each ride should have a variety of activities and will probably move to different areas for each one of them. The Pony Club Coach/Instructor might be asked to take his ride for activities such as basic equitation, jumping, stable management and an instructional hack during the course of a day rally. Alternatively he could give one session at an evening rally.

The amount of guidance as to the content of the sessions will vary, but the Chief Coach/Instructor, sometimes working through the Rally Organiser, should arrange the timetable, allocate the facilities and notify those who will be teaching as to what type of lesson or lessons they will be asked to take (mounted, dismounted, large group, small group, etc.). He may also suggest or discuss with the Coaches/Instructors what form the sessions should take. Whether mounted or dismounted, this will depend on:
• The facilities available.
• The size of the ride.
• The age and standard of the ride.
• The time available.

The following pages contain some ideas for activities—both mounted and unmounted. Try to make the best of any given situation and, if necessary, modify your prepared lessons to make them safe and enjoyable for the standard of the ride.

NOTE: The ride should always be inspected before any mounted activity begins (*see* page 35).

Forms of Instruction—Mounted

Class Lesson

This is the most valuable way of teaching basic riding on the flat and over fences.

Suitable for: Up to 8 riders.

Requirements: *See* pages 26 and 27 for diagrams of arenas.
A flat area of at least 20 x 40 m. A minimum of
4 markers, and either props for a game or a fence or
two. (Larger rides will need an area of at least
20 x 60 m., 4 corner markers and 8 other markers
(preferably letters).

Procedure: *See* page 34 for procedure, page 52 for jumping,
or, where applicable, page 41 'Sample Lessons' (for
members aged 6 to 11).

Over 12 riders: This is not recommended. It is difficult to remain
safe and achieve improvement with large
numbers of riders in a class lesson.

**Up to 5 senior
riders:**   The class lesson is essential for teaching more
advanced riders, especially those working for
'A' Test who must be given concentrated and
individual help. *See* page 123, 'Gaining More
from a Session'.

**Up to 5 younger
riders:**   Great progress can be made during a class lesson
but beware of overworking the ride. It is a
challenge to make individual concentrated work
enjoyable for the average or younger member.
Plan to teach by means of carefully selected games.
The lesson may be informal as small numbers are
easier to control. *See* page 39, 'Instructing
Beginners and the Very Young' and page 57,
'Teaching Riders to Jump'.

Instructional Hack or Country Ride

All road safety training is done OFF the public roads but the procedures for riding ON public roads may be practised on private roads, farm tracks, and in simulated road tests. The aim of riding through the country is to encourage members to ride with intelligence and consideration for others, and be aware of the pace used while hacking in various conditions. Country rides are also useful for educational purposes to gain a better understanding of the countryside and different methods of farming.

Suitable for:　　　Any size ride, but when there are more than 6 riders the coach/instructor must have a competent assistant.

Requirements:　　　A quiet horse for the Coach/Instructor to ride. With junior rides, there should be one extra helper for every 5 children—competent associates are ideal. Several leading reins.

Procedure:　　　You should have a competent rider in front, who knows the way and will set a sensible pace. Position yourself or a helper at the back, where the whole ride can be watched and problems quickly noticed.

For practice on private roads:　　　Ride on the left in groups of three or four pairs. The first pair of each group should be competent. Young ponies should be on the left of steady ponies. Leave room for two or three cars to overtake between each group. When crossing a road wait until everyone has caught up, and cross or turn as one unit.

In open country:　　　Keep control. Do not canter unless the ride is settled and safe at a trot. For the first canter, send the ride up a hill, one after another stopping before they reach the top. Impetuous ponies should go first.

NOTE:　　　Fluorescent tabards must be worn by ALL riders should the need arise to go onto the public roads.

Working a ride

Formation Riding

Suitable for: Average or large size rides.

Requirements: A flat area 20 x 40 m., or 30 x 60 m. for larger rides.
Corner markers or letters.
If riding to music, a suitable audio system.

Procedure: At first practice each movement in walk without music. Always call the movements. (*See* page 108, 'Producing a Formation Ride'.)

Mock Hunt

Suitable for: Large numbers. This can be great fun for everyone and is suitable during an afternoon at a day rally or camp.

Requirements: Permission from one or two farmers to ride through woodland and across or round some fields.
A carefully planned route marked appropriately with trails and false trails.
Sawdust, shavings or white, washable emulsion paint for laying the trails. Paper should not be used as it litters the countryside.
Plenty of mounted assistants and mobile back-up help.

Procedure: An adult should be the huntsman. Appoint members to be whippers-in, hounds, field masters, gate shutters, etc. Although the huntsman should know the route, it is more fun if he hunts the 'hounds' as realistically as possible, using his horn correctly, casting, and allowing 'hounds' to 'pick up the scent'. (*See* 'Countryside Studies and Hunting', page 84.)

Paper Chase

This is not as instructive as the mock hunt, but is easier to prepare and can be over a shorter distance.

Suitable for: A large ride or several rides joining together. An enjoyable way to end a day rally.

Requirements: As for a mock hunt. *See* previous page.

Procedure: Members should work as individuals or in pairs.

Scavenger Hunt

Useful for teaching the ride to identify trees and plants, or simply as a game.

Suitable for: Any size ride, but particularly useful for ending a lesson with large groups of younger children, perhaps working them in pairs.

Requirements: 'Planted' items or natural items growing in the area.

Procedure: Define the boundaries. Explain that items must be searched for and collected from within the defined area. Name the items to be found. If they are plants or leaves, show examples and discuss the advantages and disadvantages of having them growing in a paddock. The degree of difficulty of the items chosen should be according to the standard of the ride. The very young should play the game only at walk or trot, and should collect items which do not entail dismounting.

Gymkhana Games

These are useful for teaching the correct way of riding with the reins in one hand, mounting and dismounting from both sides at the halt, vaulting on and off while the ponies move forward, leading mounted and dismounted, etc., or for recreation at the end of a rally.

Suitable for: Any size of ride as long as you have enough props and assistants.

Requirements: Any gymkhana props. With 4 rows of bending poles, 4 buckets, 4 scarves and some paper cups, several games can be played.
If you are training the branch Prince Philip Cup team, have the appropriate props to be used in the games chosen for that year.

Procedure: Split the ride into teams, achieving a balance between the skilful and less competent riders. For ideas about games *see* the Pony Club book *Gymkhanas and Rally Games*.

Dressage Lesson

Suitable for: Smaller rides. Best with fewer than 6 riders so that each may have a chance to practise on his own in the arena.

Requirements: An accurately marked out dressage arena, 20 x 40 m., with letters and corner markers.

Procedure: *See* diagram of arena, page 27 and 'Riding a Dressage Test', page 87.

Show-Jumping Lesson

Suitable for: Average or smaller size rides.

Requirements: A course of show jumps on a flat piece of ground.

Procedure: *See* 'Show Jumping', page 91.

Cross-Country Lesson

Suitable for: Any size ride.

Requirements: A variety of cross-country fences.
A quiet horse for the Coach/Instructor
if you decide to ride.
An assistant or two depending on the size
and standard of the ride, either mounted or
in a cross-country vehicle (e.g. Land Rover).

Procedure: With less experienced riders, the Coach/Instructor
should be dismounted. (*See* 'Riding Across Country',
page 94.)

Road Safety Lesson

Suitable for: Average or smaller size rides.
(Best with fewer than 9 riders.)

Requirements: A flat area approx 100 x 60 m.
Markers and other equipment used in the Field
Test layout of the current Road Rider Test.

Procedure: *See* 'Road Safety', page 86.

Discussion

Suitable for: A break during any lesson, in a quiet, sheltered place.

Procedure: This can take place spontaneously, at any time, to give
ponies and riders a rest. With the ponies standing in a
semi-circle, choose a suitable topic, then start a
discussion, encouraging everyone to join in. Five
minutes will be ample. Do not allow the ride to get
cold. (*See* the 'Five-Minute Talk', page 78.)

Forms of Instruction—Dismounted

Practical Horse and Pony Care

The most constructive way to teach stable management, as members are shown how something should be done and then practise doing it themselves.

Suitable for: Groups of up to 8 members.

Requirements: Good quality props or the use of a well-appointed stable yard with, for example, tack in saddle room; samples of various feedstuffs in feed room; hay, straw and haylage in hay barn; horse box; grooming kit; farrier's tools; a quiet pony or members' own ponies.

Procedure: If possible, the subject should be taught in its appropriate environment. For example, explain about 'feeding' in the feed room. Then discuss storage and methods of feeding as well as identifying various feeds. It is important for everyone to do some practical work.

Smaller groups: With fewer members you will have more time, so take the opportunity to cover the subject in greater detail. (*See* 'Instruction in Horse and Pony Care', page 74).

Stable Management Tasks

This is a good way for members to learn or revise several aspects of practical stable management. Each group moves to each task point in turn.

Suitable for: 9 to 18 members.

Requirements: Three task points such as:
1. Grooming point. Quiet pony correctly tied-up; grooming kit.
2. Tack cleaning point. Sufficient tack cleaning equipment for everyone in a group; some dirty tack.
3. Saddling-up point. One or two quiet ponies correctly tied up; saddles and bridles to fit them. One Coach/Instructor or an assistant for each task point and pony.

Procedure: Brief your assistant thoroughly. They must teach each group according to its standard. Make sure that they teach the reasons why it is important for the tasks to be done well: e.g., ponies soon become nervous at the sight of their saddlery unless it is put on sympathetically. Divide the members into groups of up to 6 of a similar standard. Groups move to each task point where, after a brief demonstration, members practise the task while their Coach/ Instructor makes comments and gives advice. (*See* 'Instruction in Horse and Pony Care', page 74.)

Textbook Instruction in *The Manual of Horsemanship*

Suitable for: Teaching horsemastership or theory of equitation to average or small-sized groups with no props.

Requirements: Somewhere comfortable to sit.
Copies of *The Manual of Horsemanship*.

Procedure: Each member of the group takes a turn in reading aloud from selected pages. When necessary make interventions to elaborate on or to demonstrate a particular point. Stress the importance of reading as a means of learning.

Video or DVD

Suitable for: Groups small enough to enable everyone to have a good view of the screen.

Requirements: Viewing equipment and, if possible, a camera. Preferably a room set aside for viewing—with a TV screen which the whole class can easily see.

Suitable recordings of the ride taken during a recent lesson.

Procedure: *See* 'Using Audio Visual Equipment', page 80.

Quiz

Suitable for: Groups of any size. The gathering may be on a large scale (involving other branches, for example) when it will require considerable preparation; or it may merely be used as a way of helping a small group to learn a subject perhaps after lunch at a rally.

Requirements: A place suitable for the type and size of the gathering and for the length of the quiz.

Procedure: If you are using the quiz to teach 11 or more members at a rally or camp, form teams. Either ask the questions yourself, or arrange for everyone to read the appropriate pages of the *Manual* beforehand, and instruct each one to produce 2 questions to ask the opposing team. You could also use the *Pony Club Quiz Books*.

Lecture

Suitable for: Groups of any size. Particularly useful when teaching large numbers.

Requirements: A comfortable, quiet place where the group can sit. Visual aids.

Procedure: *See* 'Giving a Lecture', page 78.

Discussion

Suitable for: Any group at any time.

Procedure: Spontaneous discussions are appropriate either during rest times when riding, stable management sessions out of doors or in the class room. Give a short introduction, then start a discussion, perhaps by asking an individual 'How do you do this?' Discussion keeps everyone on their toes; they must all be encouraged to join in. *See* 'The Five-Minute Talk', page 78.

3   Use of the Voice

The ride should be able to hear the Coach/Instructor clearly and without effort. Most men and a large percentage of women can be easily heard. Some Coaches/Instructors have great difficulty in 'throwing' their voice and suffer very considerable stress after an hour or so of teaching. They are advised to seek professional help from a voice production teacher.

To ensure that you are heard clearly, the following points may be helpful:
• Position yourself with the ride in front of you. When out of doors, have your back to the wind.
• Look up.
• Don't shout.
• Use your lips, the tip of your tongue and your jaw actively to produce good vowel and consonant sounds.
• Speak more slowly than you normally do.
• Vary the tone and speed of your voice, to add expression and enthusiasm.
• Don't let your voice die away at the end of the sentence (this is usually due to lack of breath).
• Don't be afraid of silence. Use it! A pause is often better than repeating yourself.
• Try to relax your throat and the muscles at the back of your tongue.
• ABOVE ALL TRY TO BREATHE CORRECTLY.

How to Breathe Correctly

Breathing correctly requires some practice. First, take an especially deep breath and hold it . . . you will almost certainly have produced a total block in your throat. When you let go, your breath will rush out. This is incorrect. Instead, place your hands on either side of the ribs nearest to your waistband. Breathe slowly in, first filling the space between your hands, then letting your chest fill with air. Finally, without allowing that 'block' to happen, continue breathing out gently and smoothly, until your ribs squeeze out the last of the air, and your hands move inwards.

Do not worry if after two or three such breaths you feel dizzy or have to cough. It just means that you are using part of your lungs that haven't been used for some time. Good breathing produces a well-controlled voice which will carry.

Taking the Mounted Ride

4   Controlling the Ride During a Class Lesson

It is of vital importance for the Coach/Instructor to be confident and familiar with the simple terms of command. He will thus be at ease when controlling the ride

The Riding Area (Figs. 1, 2, 3, 4)
A ride is more easily controlled in an arena or school.
The four corners should be clearly marked, ideally with boards, otherwise with cones

It is helpful if centre, 'quarter', and half markers are correctly lettered. For competitions the centre lines, and letters D, X, G, etc, are generally marked by mowing. They are not normally marked at rallies.

If you are using an arena without letters or have merely been allocated a space in a field, use any safe objects, such as cones, or buckets with the handles removed.

Corner markers are the first priority, followed by centre, 'quarter', and half markers.

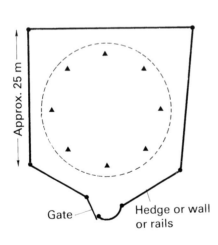

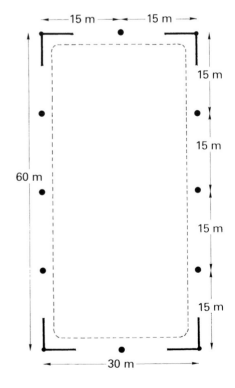

Fig. 1   Small enclosed area suitable for beginners or the very young. The track is outside the markers.

Fig. 2   An arena suitable for large rides and for formation riding. Here marked with upturned buckers or cones.

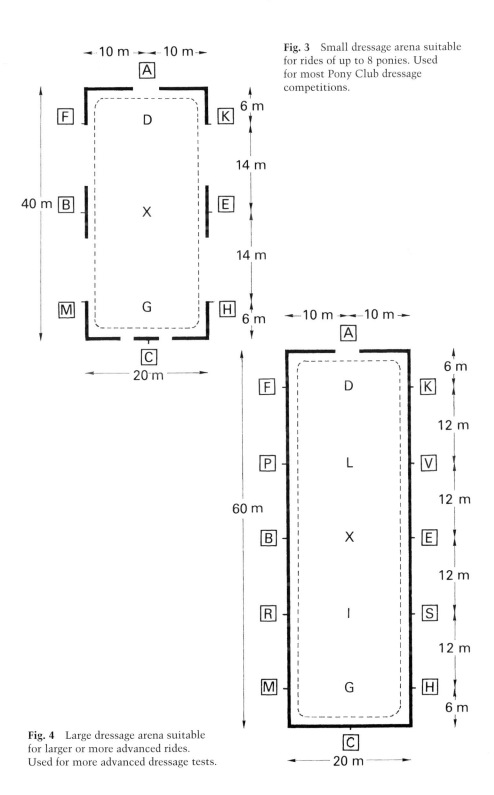

Fig. 3 Small dressage arena suitable for rides of up to 8 ponies. Used for most Pony Club dressage competitions.

Fig. 4 Large dressage arena suitable for larger or more advanced rides. Used for more advanced dressage tests.

Order of Riding

When working as a ride the rider at the front is called 'leading file'. The rider at the back is called 'rear file'.

Pace (or gait) should change only when the command is given.

Speed	The leading file sets the speed. An even, steady, regular pace should be maintained as far as possible by all ride members.
Distance	Riders are responsible for maintaining the distance between their own ponies and the heels of the pony in front. The distance is usually half a horse's length (approx. 1.5 m. or 5 ft.), but this may be varied to suit circumstances and safety.
Tracks	The outer track is just within the perimeter of the arena. The ride should stay on this track, riding the corners as quarter circles, unless told to do otherwise. The inner track should be ridden 1.5 m. inside the outer track.
Direction	*'On the right rein'* means clockwise.
	'On the left rein' means anti-clockwise.
	'Track right' means turn to the right on reaching the track.
	'Track left' means turn to the left on reaching the track.
Simple School Movements	Circles, Changes of rein*, Turns*, Loops*, Serpentines*

* These movements are described (with words of command and diagrams) on pages 30–31.

Directive Terms

'Whole ride' means all together.

'In succession' means one at a time.

'Walk on a loose rein' means gradually lengthen the reins, allowing the pony to stretch his neck forwards and down.

'Make much of your ponies' means give your ponies a rewarding pat.

'Sit at ease' means lengthen the reins so that the pony can rest while at halt.

'Go large' means return to the outer track and remain on the same rein.

Position of the Coach/Instructor

Ideally, the Coach/Instructor should place himself with his back to the wind and about 2 m. (6.5 ft.) from the track and from the centre line. From here he can watch the ride easily and will not interfere with movements, such as turns down the centre or changes of rein. He should, however, feel free to move in order to observe riders or ponies from different angles.

WORDS OF COMMAND

Words of command have three functions:
1. **WHO** is being given the command: e.g., *'Whole ride'*, 'In succession', or the rider's name, etc.
2. **WHAT** they are commanded to do: e.g., *'Prepare to trot'*.
3. **WHEN** the command must be carried out: e.g., *'Ride ter–rot'*, or *'Leading file commence'*; or 4. **WHERE** the command must be carried out: e.g., *'At the H marker'*, or *'As you cross the centre line'*. Thus the riders will know that they must either *'do it now'* (3) or *'do it later at the named place'* (4).

For example: *'Whole ride, prepare to trot'* . . . (pause) . . . *'Ride ter–rot'*. *'In succession, turn down the centre line and halt at X, then rejoin the rear of the ride'* . . . (pause) . . . *'Leading file commence'* . . . (and then). . . *'Next'*, *'Next'*, etc.

Time your commands and speak them clearly, pausing between each stage. Give the executive command (e.g., *'Leading file commence'*) when the rider has arrived at a good place to begin the exercise.

If you begin your commands too late, the riders will not have enough time to prepare, and may pass the point where the exercise is to be performed. It is better to begin too early and then pause for a few seconds before giving the final command.

The ride should act on the executive command accurately and smoothly. If the executive word is drawn out (*'ter-rot'*) rather than snapped (*'trot'*), good transitions will be encouraged. The tone of your voice will influence ponies and riders. The increase of pace should be on an upward note, and the decrease of pace on a falling note.

ALWAYS ENSURE THAT:
• The riders understand the words of command.
• They know their left from their right.
• Your leading file is competent and preferably has done school work before.

Commanding School Movements

The following terms may be used if letters are not available:
• 'Centre markers' for A and C.
• 'Quarter markers' for F, K, H and M.
• 'Half markers' for B and E.

Circles may be ridden in single file or in succession. Generally a 20-metre circle is a good size. Smaller circles can be asked for and their size carefully explained.

Sample Turns and Changes of Rein (Direction)

'In single file, at E turn right, at B track left' (Fig. 5a)
or   *'In single file, at E turn right, at B track right'*
       (to stay on the same rein Fig. 5b).

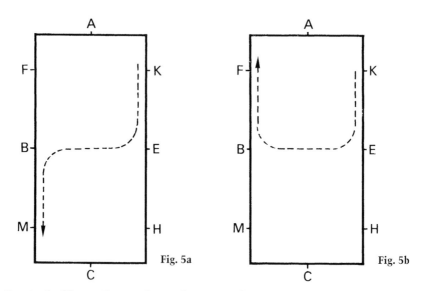

'In single file, at C turn down the centre line, at A track right' (Fig. 6a).
or *'In single file, at C turn down the centre line, at A track left'*
       (to stay on the same rein Fig. 6b).

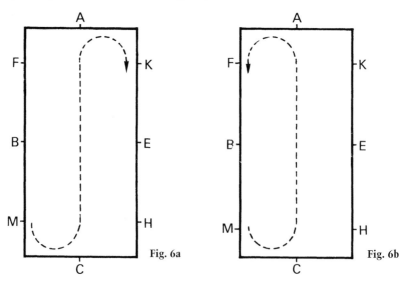

'In single file, right (or inwards) incline to change the rein from K' (Fig. 7).
'In single file, at A half-circle right to X and half-circle left to C' (Fig. 8).

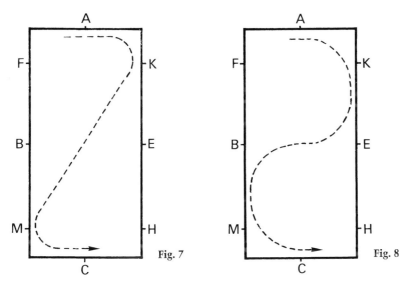

Fig. 7

Fig. 8

'In single file, ride a loop of 5 metres between F and M' (Fig. 9).
*'In single file, ride a serpentine of three large loops from A to C,
each loop touching the track'* (Fig. 10).

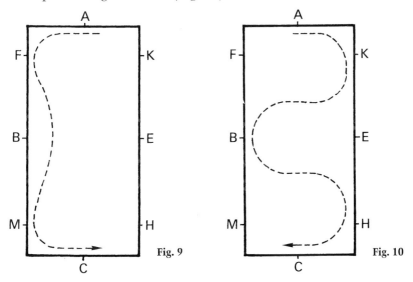

Fig. 9

Fig. 10

AVOID ENDLESS TROTTING ROUND THE ARENA

To Halt and to Move Off

(Please note that the diagrams are not drawn to scale.)

The simplest and the most expedient method in an emergency
'Whole ride, prepare to halt, ride ha–alt.'
'Whole ride, prepare to walk, walk on.'

Useful when talking or demonstrating to the ride
'Leading file, at M (or other named marker) inwards turn and halt, the remainder form a ride on his left (or right).' (Fig. 11a).

'In succession, from the right, walk and track left; walk on.' (Fig. 11b).

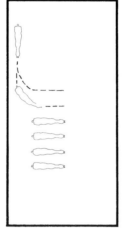

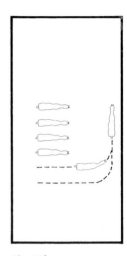

Fig. 11a   Fig. 11b

The easiest halt for the ponies
'Leading file prepare to halt; the remainder turn in and form a ride on his left (or right); leading file ha–alt.' (Fig. 12a).

'In succession, from the right (or left), prepare to walk and track left (or right); walk on.' (Fig. 12b).

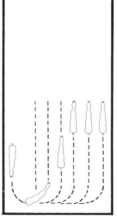
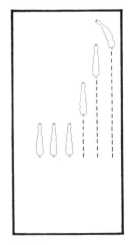

Fig. 12a   Fig. 12b

To halt, keeping the ponies well apart
'Whole ride, prepare to turn in and halt 3 metres in from the track;
ride turn'. (Fig. 13a).
'Whole ride, prepare to walk and track right (or left); walk on'. (Fig. 13b).

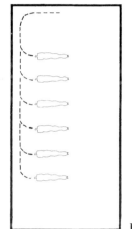 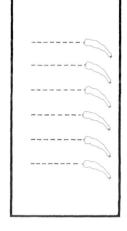

Fig. 13a   Fig. 13b

Before halting the ride, consider:
• If you are going to do a demonstration, will they be able to see?
• Will there be sufficient room in front of them?
• Will the sun be shining directly in their or your eyes?
• Can you use hedges or buildings as shelter from the elements?

School Manners and Discipline

Throughout the lesson the ride remains:
1. In single file.
2. On the outer track.
3. On the same rein.
4. The same distance apart.
5. In the basic paces (medium walk, working trot
   and working canter) until commanded otherwise.

• After completing a commanded movement, the rider should return
  to the outer track.
• If the distance between two riders becomes too great, the rider who
  is left behind should cut the arena short by turning early across the
  short side. The riders behind should follow.

- When trotting, riders should sit on the correct diagonal.
- When moving in opposite directions, riders must pass left hand to left hand.
- Whips are generally carried in the inside hand. When using a whip, care should be taken to avoid upsetting another rider's pony.
- Tongue-clicking should be discouraged.
- Consideration should be shown to other members of the ride, and riders should be taught to be attentive to the behaviour of other ponies and to act accordingly.
- The Coach/Instructor should always encourage good manners in his ride.

The above terms and disciplines are a simple means of controlling a ride safely and effectively. The Coach/Instructor who is conversant with them will be free to apply himself to the more important task of teaching.

For more ambitious ways of controlling the ride, *see* 'School Movements Performed in Various Ways: Formation Riding', page 100.

5   Procedure for Giving a Class Lesson

Before you begin you should:
- Prepare your lesson according to the information given to you in advance. (In some Branches, you will be asked to teach a certain subject; in others it will be left to your discretion).
- Inspect the area where you will be teaching.
- Check your 'props'.
- Brief your assistant (if you have one).

When taking the ride you should bear in mind the following points:
1. Try to develop good communication by asking frequent questions and by encouraging questions and comments from the ride.
2. Choose with care the time when you reach your 'lesson of the day'.
3. Members and their ponies tire quickly; therefore both need frequent periods of rest, with ponies walking on a loose rein or riders 'sitting at ease'.
4. Concentration lasts for short periods only. It must be constantly restimulated.
5. Emphasis should vary between physical effort, mental effort, excitement, and relaxation.

You might use the following outline on which to have a rally period of two hours. Because of the time taken during the preliminaries and moving to your area and back, your working time will probably be one and a half hours.

Introduction and Inspection

As a rule the Rally Organiser will allocate your ride and introduce the members to you. Before moving off, make sure that they know your name. Line them up, and make your introduction in a place where help, spare equipment, leather punch, numnahs, adult stirrups, mobile phone, etc., are close at hand.

With each rider:

- Establish a friendly rapport while you quickly make your checks.
- Ask each member his name and the name and age of his horse or pony. Ask what the horse/pony does and does not like doing.
- Find out if the animal is owned, borrowed, or hired, and if he kicks or has any other problems.
- Note the condition of the horse/pony. If he is very thin or dull, tactfully find out why. Refer any completely unsuitable animals to the DC or Rally Organiser, who should advise the parents.
- Make sure that every rider on a young horse or pony has a neckstrap. (For details on fitting the neckstrap, *see* page 39).
- Check that the rider's hat and footwear comply with the current official safety rules. Riders with unsuitable footwear should ride without stirrups, if they are safe, or borrow a spare pair.

Then:

- Check the fit and condition of saddlery. Members should not be allowed to ride with:
  1. Stirrups which are much too small (the foot can wedge) or much too large (the heel can slide through). A rider may be allowed to join in without stirrup-irons and leathers, or use a spare pair.
  2. Stirrup leathers, girths or reins with rotten leather or stitching.
  3. Girths which are too loose when on the tightest holes, try adding another numnah.
- As temporary measures, fit numnahs to saddles which are too low, and knot reins which are too long. (Make a knot at the buckle end).
- Explain that saddlery must fit correctly because no horse or pony will work properly if he is uncomfortable. As he carries his rider's weight through the saddle, its fit is obviously vital. Bridles can also cause discomfort: e.g. tight browbands pinch at the base of the ears; tight throat-lashes become too restrictive when the pony tries to relax his jaw; bits which are too long have incorrect actions.
- Be aware that the rider will have difficulty in sitting correctly in a saddle which tips too far forward, or (more common) too far back. (A good saddler can make adjustments).

- Remember that you are there to help and teach, not to judge and condemn. Correct that which is dangerous or uncomfortable, make necessary adjustments, and suggest that any lesser problems should be put right by the next rally.
- Always praise those who are well turned out.
- Refer dangerous and unsolvable problems to the DC or Rally Organiser.
- Arrange your ride in pairs, with keen ponies in front and kickers at the back. Lead them to your area at the walk.

The Riding Area is described on page 26. It should preferably be on flat, well-drained land.

Organising the Ride
Chapter 4 covers the minimum requirements. Make sure that you know where to stand and what to say. When you are more experienced and can control your ride with ease and confidence, *see* Chapter 18, 'School Movements Performed in Various Ways—Formation Riding', page 100.

Assessing and Working-In the Ride
Line up your riders side by side, facing you, with half a horse's length between them. Discuss briefly what you plan to do during the lesson.

Make sure that they check their girths and remind them to re-check after a short period of work.

See that they know the commands and expressions which you will use, and that they know their left from their right.

Work the ride on both reins at walk and trot.

Observe each horse/pony and rider carefully and form an opinion of them. This is your assessment period.

At this stage don't make too many comments—GIVE THE RIDE TIME TO SETTLE DOWN.
- Check that your leading file sets a good constant pace.
- Change the ride order if necessary.
- Use simple school movements to help the ride to supple up.
- Avoid small circles and complicated movements.
As soon as they have settled down and you have made your assessment, halt the ride.

Basic Corrections
Explain the importance of the correct position, and adjust the length of stirrup leathers if necessary. At all times the Coach/Instructor should be aware of each rider's faults and should make corrections where

necessary, constantly encouraging the rider to work on his position. (*See* 'Developing the Rider's Position', page 45). Ask the riders how they felt their horses or ponies worked.

Revise the aids, reaffirming previous lessons.

Physical Exercises
If the ponies are calm and obedient, use physical exercises to help the riders' balance and to increase their confidence. *See* page 48.

The Lesson of the Day
The right time to begin teaching your subject is about twenty minutes after the beginning of the lesson. By now the riders and ponies should be well settled down and ready to concentrate on your lesson, which should follow these basic principles:

1. **Plan:** this should be part of your advance preparation. It should include knowledge of numbers, age group, standard, and what the Branch Chief Instructor requires.
2. **Explain** what you are going to teach and why.
3. **Demonstrate** clearly how to do whatever you are teaching: this can be done by either you, your assistant, or a ride member.
4. **Practice:** the ride puts into practice what has been explained and demonstrated, completing the sequence of HEAR, SEE, FEEL. This might be carried out individually, as a ride, or in groups, depending on the movement. Ask riders to comment on their work.
5. **Correction:** comment with praise or corrections as and when you see it happening.
6. **Demonstrate again:** they may find it helpful to be shown again.
7. **Practise again**
8. **Comment again**
9. **Feedback:** confirm by questioning that they have fully understood the lesson. Be tactful with those who need further explanation. Ask riders what they need to practise.

The lesson of the day does not have to be on the flat but could well be jumping or a related subject such as 'the approach to a fence', or 'riding a track'.

During this period the maximum time should be spent by the ride *doing*, and the minimum time by the Coach/Instructor talking and demonstrating.

Be quick to observe the good or the not so good, and comment on them accordingly. If you can give the rider the 'feel' and understanding of what is correct, you will have taught a good lesson.

Period of Relaxation

After the period of concentration or exertion there should be a short break, when you can discuss an item of interest (e.g. *'Do you all know the name of your pony's bit and what it is made of?'*), or play a quiet game (e.g. equestrian items beginning with certain letters of the alphabet). (*See* 'The Five-Minute Talk', page 78.)

Jumping

Most members will feel deprived if there is no jumping at a rally, but occasionally there may be children who don't enjoy it. Be aware of this minority and do not force or frighten them.

Jumping may take many forms and can be related to the lesson of the day. Some suggestions are:

- The single fence.
- The double or treble fence.
- A course of jumps.
- A cross-country ride including natural fences.
- Cross-country fences.
- Jumping up and down hill.
- Ditches.
- Jumping without stirrups.

This is also a good opportunity to explain how to put up safe jumps at home. (For more detailed ideas *see* 'Jumping Exercises Needing a Small Amount of Equipment' page 67).

Games

Depending on the time available, how much work the ponies have done, and how tired the riders are, it can be fun to play a game. Even quite senior riders enjoy this; the ponies certainly do. It is a good idea to relate the game to the lesson which you have taught, such as:

Turns and Circles	Bending
Mounting and Dismounting	Musical Sacks
The Approach to a Fence	The Stride Game. (The rider counts forwards during the approach to a fence.) *See* page 69.
Altering Stirrups	A team race. Start at normal length, ride to far end, shorten stirrup leathers, and return over small jumps.
Cross-Country Ride	'I Spy', with flora and fauna.

...Or else you may use your ingenuity to come up with other games.

Ending the Lesson / Warm Down

It is important for the ponies to be cool by the end of the lesson, as they may be travelling home by box, or standing tied up for the next part of the rally.

Spend the final few minutes reaffirming the important points learned and reminding each individual of the things they must remember and practise before the next rally.

Give back any whips or other items which you have taken from the riders. Make sure that any borrowed numnahs, etc., are returned. Then walk the ride safely back to 'base', and report progress to the DC or Rally Organiser.

Reflection / Self-Evaluation

Lastly, make a mental or written note of how successful the rally was and how it might have been improved. Reflect not only on what you taught, but on how you taught it. Everyone makes mistakes. Try to learn from both the good and the less successful parts of your programme.

6   Instructing Beginners and the Very Young

Extra Items Which Will Be Required

- Neckstraps
- String to make grass-reins
- Props for games

Every beginner should have a **neckstrap**. Either a narrow stirrup leather or a shortened martingale strap is best. Fit the neckstrap so that it rests one-third of the way up the pony's neck where the rider can hold it in an emergency or, later, when learning to jump. A piece of string may be fitted from the front 'D' on the saddle to the neckstrap, to prevent it from slipping forward if the pony lowers his head. Make sure that borrowed neckstraps are returned to you after the rally.

Grass reins prevent a pony from grazing while being ridden. There are various ways of fitting them, e.g.

1. Run a piece of string from the front 'D' of the saddle through the back of the noseband and back to the 'D' on the other side.
2. Run two pieces of string from the front 'D' of the saddle down through the loop of the browband to the ring of the bit. The pony must be free to use his head and neck. Fit the grass-reins so that he can stretch his nose to within at least 18 in., (46 cm.) of the ground but is not able to try to eat the grass.

Make sure that you have a supply of **props**, such as cones or safe markers and other items that you will need to play the games you have planned.

Extra Saddlery to Be Checked

As well as the normal inspection described on page 35, check:

1. **Stirrup bars** in the form of a fixed 'D'. When stirrup leathers are attached through a fixed 'D' (often found on felt saddles) *safety stirrups* must be used.
2. **Reins** should be narrow to fit children with small fingers.

Special Considerations when Taking the Ride:

- Remember that these young and inexperienced riders must not be frightened; are unable to concentrate for long; and must enjoy themselves—learning through games. SAFETY is a prime consideration.
- The Coach/Instructor should be dismounted.
- An enclosed area is essential (*See* Fig. 1 on page 26.) Check that the gate is shut.
- Make the area approx. 25 x 25 m., or adaptable to the number of riders and the size of their animals.
- Some of the ponies may be on leading-reins. In any case, have plenty of competent dismounted assistants.
- Work the ride on the outside of the markers as this will make the track a better shape and will stop the ponies cutting in.
- If numbers are few, it is sometimes easier to halt the ride on the track in single file rather than facing inwards.
- The first priority is to help each rider to feel confident, happy with his pony and 'at home' on his pony's back.

Keep the working-in period short, and then correct the riders' positions, adjusting stirrup leather lengths if necessary.

All beginners feel more secure with slightly short leathers. But do not allow them to ride on the backs of their saddles.

Those who have difficulty in holding their reins at the correct length can sometimes be helped by marking with rubber bands the places where each hand should be.

The lesson of the day should be simple and easily remembered. Sample lessons follow on the next few pages.

To practise what you have taught, get the ride moving as soon as possible. Then play a few carefully selected games which incorporate what you have been teaching. The games need not be competitive as not all children want to compete.

Sample Lessons

The following sample lessons are intended for members aged 6 to 11, but may be adapted for older, inexperienced members. The lessons are progressive.

Moving Off and Stopping

Suitable for a pre-D ride on or off the leading-rein. You should be dismounted, but borrow a demonstrator, perhaps from a more experienced ride.

1. **Plan your lesson** bearing in mind the age of the riders, and also the devious behaviour of some of the ponies.
2. **Explain:** after assessing the ride and working-in, line up the riders and discuss with them that today you are going to teach them how to move off and halt correctly, which will make it easier for them to control their ponies; ponies are more obedient when they are given clear aids.
3. **Demonstrate:**   (a) Preparing to walk.
    (b) How some ponies will move from a very light aid.
    (c) What to do if a stronger aid is needed.
    (d) How to guide the pony.
    (e) How to stop with the minimum of fuss.
4. **Practise:** from where they are standing as a ride, they should prepare to walk, and walk forward in succession. You can then make a comment to each one. Once on the track, in single file, they can practise halting and moving off as a ride. Later they might practise in pairs or with the whole ride abreast up the length of the school.
5. **Correct** or praise at the relevant moment. Always try to be helpful and encouraging.
6. **Reaffirm** by playing games such as 'Simon says' or 'Grandmother's footsteps', which involve moving off and halting. End the game by demonstrating correctly the smooth way to move off and halt.

Turns and Circles

Suitable for a pre-D standard ride, on or off the leading-rein. Be dismounted and, if possible, have a mounted assistant, perhaps a Junior Coach/Instructor. You will need some safe markers.
1. **Plan** the whole lesson beforehand.

2. **Explain:** after inspecting the ride and working-in, line up the riders and tell them that today they will learn to turn their ponies correctly and that they will use markers to help them. If you have enough helpers to hold the ponies, let the ride dismount and help you to set out pairs of markers to make a path on a straight line, round a half-circle (about 5 m. in diameter) and back down a straight line (Fig. 14). Let the ride run down the track on foot. Tell them to look where they are going.

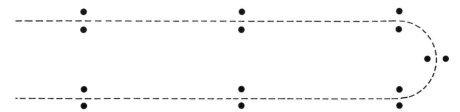

Fig. 14 'The Path.'

3. **Demonstrate** how a pony should walk down a path, round the corner, and back again, looking where he is going. Show how the rider should use his legs to keep the pony on the path along the straight parts and should use an open rein while turning.
4. **Practise**, perhaps by playing a game called 'Hannibal' in which the path is a narrow mountain track. Anyone who knocks down a marker has fallen off the track and must start again. With the demonstrator (e.g. Hannibal) as leading file the ride should, at first, go round the outer track, and then along the marked path. Change the rein. Insist on correct distances between each pony throughout the exercise.
5. **Correct** when necessary, but always be encouraging.
6. **Demonstrate again** in the form of a game. The demonstrator makes deliberate mistakes, such as showing what happens if the rider pulls too much on one rein. Members of the ride spot the mistakes and correct them. Then demonstrate the correct way to turn.
7. **Play a team game:** for example, divide the ride into two teams, each with its own 'Hannibal'. While one team practises the exercise, as (4) above, on one rein, the other team watches and makes comments. Next the second team performs while the first team watches. Then in turn, they both do the exercise on the other rein. Award marks, or have some way of making the game exciting. The winning team is the one which gets to the 'top of the mountain' with fewest casualties.

Rising Trot

Be dismounted, but have a mounted demonstrator, perhaps one member of the ride who is more advanced and can do a reasonable rising trot. It is helpful to have a few dismounted assistants.

1. **Plan your lesson** according to the age and standard of the ride.
2. After inspecting the ride and working-in, line up the riders, and by asking questions such as *'Has your pony got a bumpy trot?'* or *'How do you feel when he is trotting?'* **explain** rising trot. Tell them that they are going to perform some rising and some sitting trots.
3. **Demonstrate:**   (a) How to ask the pony to trot.
                        (b) Sitting trot.
                        (c) Rising trot.
   Explain that rising trot is more comfortable for the pony and the rider, especially when riding long distances. During the demonstration tell them to call *'One-two, one-two . . .'* in time with the sitting trot, and *'Up-down, up-down . . .'* in time with the rising trot.
4. At the halt, let the ride **practise** 'going up-down' (forward and down to help them to stay in balance) in the rhythm of the trot. Some riders may need to hold their neckstraps.
5. While the ride walks round the school, the leading file trots down the long side, showing a few strides of sitting trot and then rising. The less experienced should be led by an assistant, who should watch the rider and be ready to steady him if necessary.
6. **Make corrections** and give plenty of encouragement.
7. **Play a game**—for example, a relay—which need not be a race. Divide the ride into 2 teams. One member of each team walks to a marker, turns around it, and comes back at rising trot. As he reaches the team, the next one starts, and so on.

Once the ride is confident at rising trot, give a lesson on diagonals. Mark one diagonal pair of legs on the demonstrator's pony, using boots or bandages of the same colour: it is then easier for the ride to see how the legs move.

Transition to Canter

Either give your own demonstrations or bring in a demonstrator, perhaps borrowed from a more experienced ride. To help the ride to see how the legs move, use three differently coloured bandages. The left canter will be clearly seen if the horse's legs are marked as follows: near-fore colour = 1; off-fore and near-hind colour = 2; off-hind colour = 3.

1. **Plan the lesson**, referring to the *Manual of Horsemanship*. Keep it simple.
2. After the introduction and working-in, line the riders up at one end of the area and teach your main subject or 'lesson of the day', first explaining that this will show how the pony canters; the aids for the transition to canter; and how the rider should sit.
3. **Demonstrate** the canter and the transitions on a large circle at the far end of the area. Ask questions like 'Which foreleg is leading?', to make the ride watch carefully, and learn by watching, Show the canter on the other rein. Confirm that the canter is in three beats, with the inside foreleg leading.
   Emphasise the following: (a) The previous pace.
                                              (b) The easiest place to make the transition.
                                              (c) The aids.
                                              (d) The position of the rider's body.
4. **Practise.** Move the ride off round the area, at the walk. Each leading file in turn should trot and then canter as demonstrated, to join the rear of the ride. A few strides of canter are sufficient to begin with. Make a comment to each rider. Correct when necessary.
5. **Change the rein and repeat.**
6. **Feedback.** Ask the riders what they felt about their transitions.
7. **Play a game:** for example, 'Space Shuttles' (Fig. 15). The ride forms a large circle with the ponies' tails to the centre. Explain that the circle is in the earth and that each rider is on a launching pad which has room for one only. Then, for example, send 'Spacecraft Jane' to 'Spacecraft Richard's pad, orbiting left'. Jane then walks forward, turns left out of the circle, trots, and then canters round the outside of the circle. On approaching the opposite side of the circle to Richard, she trots and walks. As she goes across the circle and up behind Richard, he walks out, and might be told 'Spaceship Richard' to 'Spaceship Mary, orbit right'. Then 'Spaceship Mary' to '....', etc.

   Remind the ride that space shuttles are launched and docked slowly and with great precision (walking) and that they only go fast (canter) while in orbit. This game has many variations; and other planets can be visited, etc.

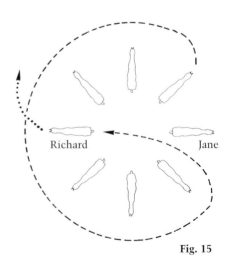

Fig. 15

7   Developing the Rider's Position

The correct position in the saddle is the essential basis for good riding and applying the aids effectively. It is most important for the Coach/Instructor to read and understand fully 'The Position of the Rider in the Saddle' (*Manual of Horsemanship*).

The development of the correct position will take time. First the beginner should acquire feel and understanding for the pony, a living creature. Secondly he should begin to find his balance while riding. Balance cannot be taught, but the Coach/Instructor can help by encouraging each rider to find his own balanced position. At this stage, games and general fun are of more value than formal class lessons.

Without making the rider stiff or inhibited, the Coach/Instructor should demonstrate the correct position and should make corrections to basic faults such as crookedness.

The Coach/Instructor should foresee and avoid the risk of falls or frightening experiences, as they destroy the rider's natural suppleness and ease. Young riders who are growing fast are prone to setbacks; a balanced position during one holiday can become an uncoordinated disaster the next. The Coach/Instructor must be sympathetic and must not allow the rider to become despondent. Awkward stages soon pass.

As balance and coordination improve, the rider will be able to feel almost a part of the horse. While retaining mobility of the hip joints and a supple back, his muscle control will develop so that he will be secure without excessive tension. Now he will be capable of applying the aids as he wishes, to direct or correct the horse. He will no longer give the wrong aids because he has lost his balance. The Coach/Instructor may then teach the correct contact of the rein and the more precise use of the leg and rein aids.

Once the rider is balanced, straight, supple and secure, he will have developed a good position.

Teaching the Correct Position
This is an important part of most lessons. The following procedure might be useful during a lesson with a less experienced ride.
1. **Explain** why it is important to sit correctly, so that it is easy for the pony to carry the rider and to obey his aids. The aim of every rider should be to achieve a balanced, supple, and secure position. He will then be able to ride effectively and in harmony with his pony. At all stages encourage the ride to comment on their own positions.

2. **Demonstrate** the correct position at the halt. It may help to show some common faults: the 'chair' seat and the 'fork' seat are obvious examples. (*See* Figs. 16, 17.) Explain why they make the rider less effective. Re-demonstrate the correct position.
3. **Check** each rider individually. Adjust stirrup leather lengths if necessary, check that they are of equal length, unless the rider has a physical defect which necessitates uneven leathers. Correct any basic faults. It is sometimes helpful to ask the rider to stand up in the stirrups after checking that the balls of his feet are on the stirrups. With supple knees and ankles, the rider will find his balance and what will generally be his correct leg position. If he then sits down gently into the saddle without moving his legs, he will be balanced, secure and comfortable.
4. **Practise:** as soon as possible have the ride moving. Depending on the standard of the ride, practice might be in the form of a game, or a series of movements incorporating one or more paces.
5. **Observe** the riders from the side and from behind. Do not hurry your assessment, as riders sometimes take time to settle down. It helps to consider the following:
   a) Is each rider in control of his pony under the given circumstances?
   b) Is he in balance with his pony?
   c) Is he straight?
   d) Is he secure without undue tension?

Fig. 16 'Fork' seat. Incorrect   **Fig. 17** 'Chair' seat. Incorrect   **Fig. 18** Correct position

6. **Correct:** when noticing a fault in the rider's position, look for the root cause rather than the obvious effect. Most faults are caused by lack of balance: e.g., the rider with bouncing hands in rising trot will almost certainly be too tense through lack of balance. There would be no point in telling him to control his hands; he must first develop a balanced position. He will then be able to be more supple in his hips, back, and shoulders, which will lead to steadier hands. This will take time and practice. Anxiety and trying too hard will only inhibit progress. There is no immediate remedy, but physical exercises, particularly numbers 3 and 6, page 49 will help.

Riders should be asked to work only on one fault at a time. A long list of faults to be corrected is of little value. Often when the basic fault is corrected the whole position will improve. Figs. 16, 17 and 19 show some common position faults. Figs. 18 and 20 show good positions.

TEACH THROUGH ENCOURAGEMENT RATHER THAN CRITICISM.

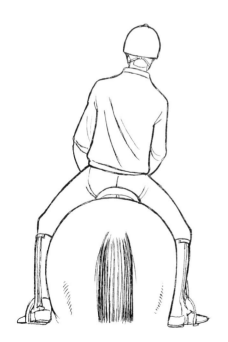

Fig. 19 Crooked seat. Incorrect

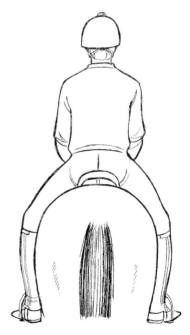

Fig. 20 Sitting straight. Correct

8   Physical Exercises

The object of physical exercises is to improve the rider's balance and security, thereby increasing confidence. In most cases this is achieved by helping the rider to control the degree of relaxation and tension in individual muscles and joints, leading to a tension-free position of the body as a whole.

Physical exercises for a short period of the lesson are fun and useful to the ride provided that:

- The horses/ponies are settled and quiet enough to be safe.
- The ride is given frequent short intervals of rest, during and between each exercise. Use the period of relaxation between exercises to explain the next exercise.
- The exercises chosen are suitable for the age and standard of the ride.
- They come at an appropriate time in the lesson.

Junior rides enjoy them during or towards the end of the lesson. Have plenty of help to lead the ponies, and to steady the riders.

Traditional favourites such as 'round the world', 'scissors', leaning forward on the pony's neck, lying back on his rump, kneeling on the saddle, etc., are performed at the halt. These are taught at most rallies and are not described here.

Middle and senior rides find exercises beneficial after the working-in period when the ponies are settled and will cooperate by moving slowly and rhythmically.

Work without stirrups will be more comfortable if the stirrup leather buckles are pulled down about 4 in. (10 cm.) from the stirrup bars before crossing the stirrups over the withers.

NOTE: Some ponies may be nervous when their riders stretch their arms high, or move in an unusual way, If you are unsure how the ponies will react, start with exercise 3(a) below before doing work without stirrups.

A Few Exercises Used for Specific Purposes

1. **To ease tension in the neck.**
   Using stirrups and with both hands on the reins, the rider turns his head slowly from side to side. The rest of his body remains in the correct position.
2. **To stretch the arms, legs and back.**
   At the halt or walk, with one hand on the reins, and without

stirrups, the rider slowly stretches his free arm up as high as he can, at the same time stretching his legs down, with his toes as low as possible. He rests, changes his rein over, and repeats the exercise with the other arm.

3. **To ease tension and to straighten the shoulders.**
   (a) Using stirrups and with the reins in one hand, the rider lets his free arm hang by his side. He then swings it rhythmically forwards, backwards, forwards, up and over. He repeats the exercise, rests, changes his reins over, and practises with the other arm.
   (b) Walking on a loose rein, the rider shrugs his shoulders and then rests. He repeats this several times.
   (c)* At the halt or walk, with stirrups and with reins knotted on the pony's neck, the rider sits up straight with his hands on his waist. He swings his left elbow and shoulder forwards three times, allowing the right elbow and shoulder to go back, but keeping his head straight. He then swings his right elbow and shoulder forwards and repeats the exercise several times.

4.* **To exercise the muscles in the waist.**
   ('Aeroplanes'.) At the halt or walk, with stirrups, but with the reins knotted on the pony's neck, the rider stretches his arms out at shoulder height. He turns his upper body including his head, quite slowly from side to side.

5. **To ease tension in the ankle-joints and to open the hips.**
   At the walk, on a long rein, without stirrups, the rider turns his toes up, in, down, and out, in a smooth circular movement of the ankles.

6. **To ease tension in the lower part of the back and the hip-joints.**
   (a) Sitting trot without stirrups. At first the rider may hook one or two fingers under the front arch of the saddle to give him confidence and to get the feel of sitting in rhythm and in balance with the pony. He should concentrate on keeping his loins and hips supple to absorb the movement. His knees and ankles should be relaxed and he should keep his lower legs well down.
       As this exercise is strenuous, give the ride frequent periods of rest. Check each rider's position carefully, watching particularly for gripping upwards with the back of the calf, which is wrong. Correct those who bump instead of sitting down in the centre of their saddles.
   (b) Without stirrups, in walk or sitting trot, the outside hand on the reins, the rider touches his inside toe with his inside hand without altering his feet position. It should be done on both reins.

* Exercises 3(c) and 4 should be carried out with discretion and only in an enclosed space.

7. **To attain a deeper seat by opening the hips and riding with the thigh flat against the saddle.** This is carried out at the halt or walk, without stirrups. With his outside hand holding the reins, the fingers of his inside hand under the saddle arch, the rider opens his legs (thighs and knees) slightly away from the saddle, draws them slightly back, and returns them to the saddle as they move forward, so that the large muscle under the thigh is pressed back behind the thigh, allowing it to lie flat on the saddle. Many riders, particularly those with round thighs, use this exercise while riding with or without stirrups, to correct their positions.

8. **To ease tension in the knees.**
At the walk on a long rein, without stirrups, the rider swings his lower legs (from the knee down) alternately forwards and backwards. His lower legs should be free from the pony's sides and he should maintain a low, still knee position on the saddle.

Checks to Be Made During Exercises

1. Each rider must understand how to do the exercise properly. It may be helpful to discuss, demonstrate, and practise the exercises at the halt, before trying them at the walk or trot.

2. Except for the part of him involved in the exercise, the rider must not compromise his correct basic position: e.g., when swinging one arm, the rest of his body should remain square with his weight carried equally on both seat bones. His seat and legs should be in the correct position and he should take care not to make any inadvertent movements.

3. The rider must not use his reins as a lifeline, even in an emergency. Should he lose his balance, he may hold on by the saddle-arch, the mane or a neckstrap, but *never* by the reins.

Exercises become more difficult if practised without stirrups or at a faster pace, e.g. trot instead of walk. Use them according to the standard of the ride. Additional exercises for work on the lunge are on page 125.

Jumping

9   Jumping

The Aims of the Coach/Instructor

1. **To Ensure Safety**
   Double-check tack. See that hats fit correctly. Knot reins which are too long. Neckstraps (for details on fitting, *see* page 39) should be used for beginners who might otherwise pull the pony in the mouth during the unaccustomed feel of the take-off. Ensure that poles are smooth and that metal fittings are removed from stands unless poles are resting on them. It is safest to give the jumping lesson in an enclosed area. Remember to shut the gate. Use your common sense to ward off a potentially dangerous situation before an accident happens. Suitable striding between fences is in the Appendix, page 164.

2. **To Instil Confidence**
   Confidence is laboriously built but easily destroyed. It is important to avoid falls. Ponies jump best over fences which look solid, imposing and inviting. Ground lines are helpful. Plan the lesson so that steady progress is made, with the most challenging fences or problems tackled three-quarters of the way through the lesson. There will then be time to correct mistakes and restore confidence if necessary.

3. **To Make Improvement**
   Riding over fences is usually improved by correcting riding faults, and by improving the quality of work on the flat. It is unnecessary and a waste of time to find out how high each pony can jump. The ride should not be over-faced, but enough interesting problems should be solved to leave the riders with a sense of achievement.

The Position of the Ride and the Coach/Instuctor

Jumping lessons consist of work on the flat and jumping. The position of the Coach/Instructor and the ride during work on the flat is covered on page 28.

When the novice ride is jumping, with few exceptions, each member will perform individually.

It is important, especially when taking a less experienced ride, for the Coach/Instructor to keep an eye on the ride as well as to watch the member who is practising.

The following diagrams show situations where single fences are in use, but the same principles apply when the Coach/Instructor is using further fences, trotting-poles, or gymnastic jumps.

The riders should be told the shape of the whole exercise, where to go and at what pace, from the time their turn starts until they rejoin the ride.

When taking more experienced rides the Coach/Instructor should suggest independent work for the riders between turns.

With less advanced riders, those who are waiting for their turns should stand still in a ride, and may be asked for comment, thus learning by watching. When standing the ponies may nod off, so the ride may be better walking a small circle.

Island Fences

The ride is positioned where it can watch, and the Coach/Instructor stands on the opposite side of the fence.

Fig. 21 shows the positioning of the ride and the Coach/Instructor, and the shape of a basic exercise, with the correct line of approach coming off a half-circle to the centre of the fence.

Fence Alongside a Hedge

Sometimes the fence is flush against a hedge or the wall of an indoor school. This is an advantage for junior riders as it helps them to keep their ponies straight. Check that the ponies cannot run out between the hedge and the fence, and build a wing on the open side of the fence. The Coach/Instructor must still be in a position to watch the performing member and the rest of the ride. This may mean changing the normal sitings of the ride.

Pairs of markers are helpful in keeping the very young on the correct lines before and after the fence. Cones are ideal, but heavy upturned plastic buckets with handles removed are a good substitute.

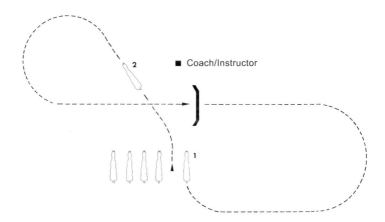

Fig. 21 The positioning of a ride using an island fence.

Fig. 22 illustrates the positioning of the ride and the Coach/Instructor when the fence is against a hedge or wall. The exercise shown is suitable for junior riders, with the markers ensuring a correct line.

A Junior Ride

If the ride is large, there will be a considerable lapse of time between a pony's first jump and his next. During this period he may get cold and stiff, and the result may well be an unnecessary stop. The following technique (shown in Fig. 23) overcomes the problem and enables two ponies to work at the same time.

(a) Riders 1 and 2 are sent out to ride at the trot in a circle.
(b) On command, rider 1 peels off the circle, jumps the fence, goes straight forward 8 to 10 yd. (7 to 9 m.), and halts. There is always a danger that on landing a pony will turn sharply to hurry back to the ride. The Coach/Instructor must insist that the pony is ridden straight forward so that the rider will learn to be in control on the landing side of the fence. The danger of a slip-up and fall will thus be avoided. The pony's presence on the far side of a fence acts as a 'carrot' to Rider 2's pony. Rider 3 moves out to trot round behind Rider 2.
(c) Rider 2, in turn, lands over the fence and replaces Rider 1, who moves off to take up his original place in the ride. Rider 4 will have moved out behind Rider 3. Continue this until all have jumped.

The Coach/Instructor can make comments to riders either when they have halted or when they return to the ride.

A Large, More Competent Ride

Follow the same procedure as that for junior riders but, according to circumstances, keep the whole ride on the move in a large circle at walk or trot when not jumping.

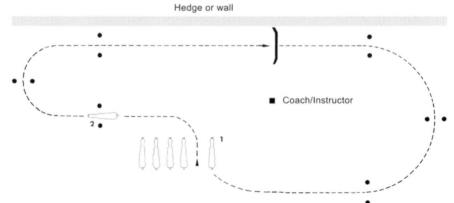

Fig. 22 The positioning of a ride using a fence alongside a hedge.

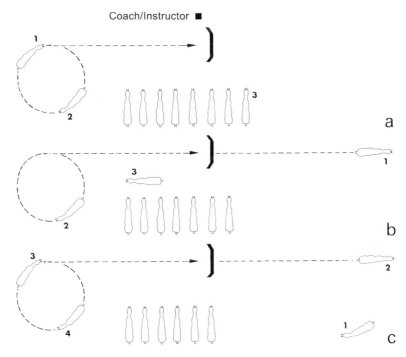

Fig. 23 A useful way of working a junior ride.

ALWAYS MAKE A CONSTRUCTIVE COMMENT TO EACH RIDER
AFTER THEIR TURN.

Planning the Jumping Lesson

1. Keep your 'aims'—to ensure safety, instil confidence, bring about
   improvement and have fun—firmly in mind.
2. Explain why jumping lessons do not consist entirely of jumping.
3. Use the structure as described in 'Procedure' on page 34.
4. Plan to include circles and other movements designed to make the ponies
   balanced, supple and obedient at the beginning of and during the lesson.
5. Remember that it is important to keep working on the riders'
   positions. (*See* 'The Rider's Position when Jumping', page 59).
6. When instructing large numbers use shorter exercises so that there
   is less time for each rider to wait between turns.

The *quality of jumping for the pony* depends on the quality of flat work
between fences.

The *quality of jumping for the rider* depends on his ability to produce
good work on the flat between the fences and to stay secure, balanced
and in good harmony with his pony at all times including the approach,
jump and recovery. Video used correctly is helpful. (*See* pages 80–82.)

Taking the Jumping Lesson

If the ride has reached the stage when stirrup leathers are to be shortened for jumping, this should be done at the beginning of the lesson.

Assessing the ride by its work on the flat can be misleading. Many ponies and riders will change their attitudes and their balance at the sight of a fence.

With juniors, walk the ride, about six ponies' lengths from each other, on a loose rein over a single pole on the ground. The ponies who break into a trot, or in other ways play up, when they see the pole will probably rush when faced with a fence. Those who trip over the pole may well prove to be sluggish.

With average and senior rides, after working in the ride, introduce a small but solid-looking fence. Do not use a wall or a fence with a fixed base until you know the capabilities of the ride. At first they should jump from the trot. One or two canter strides before and after the fence are permissible. The way the ride performs this simple exercise will indicate how the ponies and riders react to jumping.

With all but the beginners' rides, treat schooling fences as part of a movement on the flat so that they are negotiated with the minimum amount of fuss.

- Work on perfecting the whole movement, not merely the jump.
- Two fences incorporated into a movement help the rider to establish a rhythmical canter between fences.
- Aim to teach a smooth, balanced rhythmical approach, impulsive enough to jump the height required. The pony will then make his own arrangements to arrive at the correct spot for take-off. Although the development of an 'eye for a stride' is desirable especially in show jumping, when accuracy is at a premium—erratic attempts to 'find a stride' will usually end in disaster, until the rider can adjust the length of stride without upsetting the pony's rhythm and balance.
- Check that each member can produce a pace of sufficient energy to jump the fence. More energy is needed when the fence is on an uphill gradient. Heavy ponies need more energy than light ones.
- Know when to stop. Finish jumping *before* ponies and riders get tired and their work deteriorates.
- Reserve some time for ensuring the success of the last exercise and for cooling off the ponies. The lesson should finish on a happy note.
- See that the ponies are rewarded for good work. A word spoken kindly or a pat on the neck helps to settle a nervous pony, boosts confidence, and confirms in the pony's mind that he has done well, provided that the reward is given immediately after the good work.

- Members of more advanced rides should dismount immediately after halting from the final, successful, exercise, and warm down as this equates in the ponies' minds the reward—which is the relief from carrying weight—with the correct way of going.
- Whenever it is practical, all rides should dismount and lead in.
- If the last exercise is strenuous or involves galloping, more warm down time will be needed.

Teaching Riders to Jump

1. Read 'Instructing Beginners and the Very Young', page 39.
2. Neckstraps should be used. (For fitting, *see* page 39.)
3. As the pony jumps, and on landing, the rider should have little contact through the reins until the position is established sufficiently for the contact to be consistent and sympathetic.
4. In the meantime, teach the riders what to do when their ponies jump. Demonstrate at the halt how the riders should:
   - Look straight ahead.
   - Hold the neckstrap.
   - Swing forward from the hips.
5. After practising this at the halt, try it at the walk over two poles on the ground about 6 m. (20 ft.) apart, preferably alongside a hedge or fence. Put out markers in pairs to show the correct lines of approach. (*See* Fig. 22.)
6. It is useful to have helpers at the beginning and end of the approach, especially if some members of the ride are just off the leading-rein.
7. Demonstrate, or send an assistant to demonstrate, the 'course' through the markers and over the poles. Show how each rider will perform the three actions described above, as the ponies walk over the poles. The ride may then practise individually.
8. Ask the ride to point out if the member who is performing fails to carry out any of the three actions. This will hold their attention and teach them to learn by observing what others do.
9. The ride may be advanced enough to trot or to canter over a small obstacle, with a ground-line, alongside the fence or hedge. The ponies will make a hop or a small jump.
10. At this stage retain the markers and the helpers, because riders must concentrate on keeping in harmony with their ponies as they jump.
11. End the pre-jumping lesson with a game, such as 'Pass the Password', in which the poles must be negotiated, as part of a course set out with the markers, before the password can be given to the next 'messenger'.

12. Those who are able to jump small fences may finish with a game such as 'Relay'. Each rider trots away from the ride, turns round a helper, and trots back over a low fence. The next one starts immediately, as if practising for a relay race.
13. Ensure that the riders learn to reward their ponies by patting them, either soon after landing, or—if that would be unsafe—on returning to the ride.

NOTE: With just three actions to carry out, the beginner will, from the start, assume a correct position, and should never have such problems as making strange contortions or fixing the hands as the pony jumps, remembering: LOOK *forward*, HANDS *forward*, SWING *forward*.

Encouraging Ponies to Jump Well

Riders and ponies influence each other. If the pony is performing calmly and fluently, it is easier to teach the rider. Use the following points to encourage every pony to jump well.

a) Ponies jump more correctly in a flat area over a solid-looking fence with a ground-line on the take-off side. Fences should therefore be built with substantial top rails, ground-lines, and a diagonal pole or cross-poles between the two (Fig. 24).
b) Less substantial fences are needed for small ponies, which may otherwise tend to jump too high for their small riders.
c) Less experienced rides may need a 'carrot' on the landing side of the fence.
d) It sometimes helps to give a pony a lead, but choose a reliable one.
e) The best approach is usually from a large half-circle on to a straight line, to the centre of the fence. The length of the straight line may be varied. Impetuous ponies jump best off a short approach.

Having identified the lazy and the impetuous, treat them accordingly. Encourage the riders in particular to concentrate on improving their riding rather than worrying about their ponies' problems. As they improve themselves, they will automatically improve their ponies, and be able to do more demanding work.

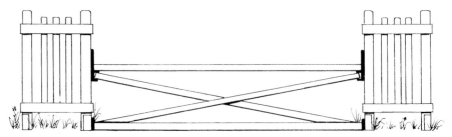

Fig. 24 A good schooling fence.

10 The Rider's Position When Jumping

The rider's basic position does not change for jumping. After each rider's position has been assessed, the stirrup leathers should be shortened if necessary. This will close the angles at the hips, knees and ankles, which increases the security of the riders and helps them to stay in balance as their ponies jump. Novice riders already ride short; it may be unsafe to shorten their stirrups further.

See *The Manual of Horsemanship*: 'Analysis of the Jump', and 'The Rider's Position for Jumping'.

Developing the Rider's Position When Jumping

The correct position is developed over a period of months or even years, first by acquiring a secure but tension-free position when riding on the flat. This enables the rider to control the approach, in both the quality of the pace and the accuracy of the chosen track or path to the fence and after it.

With practice, the rider becomes familiar with the feel of jumping, by:
(a) Swinging forward from the hips to reciprocate the thrust of the take-off.
(b) Allowing with the hands (also elbows and shoulders if necessary) as the pony's head and neck stretch forward.
(c) Absorbing most of the shock through knees and ankles as the pony lands.
(d) Remaining in balance, while the recovery stride leads to the reestablishment of the pace used in the approach.

The beginner must firstly develop confidence and balance by riding to, over, and away from very small fences.

At first the neckstrap can be held before the take-off. Later it can be held during the take-off. Eventually the rider will be secure enough to jump without the neckstrap, keeping a light contact with the reins. By now the rider's legs will be more effective and he will be able to learn how to improve his pony's paces.

He can now be taught how to make a correct, energetic approach, which will improve the quality of the pony's jump. Ideally this is the path along which progress should be made, but only too often the Coach/Instructor will be confronted by riders and ponies whose problems require long term retraining.

The following pages contain some of the more common problems with suggestions for immediate action by the Coach/Instructor.

Common Problems in the Approach

1. Rider allowing pony to rush his fences

PROBLEM (a): The rider is left behind the movement, his loss of balance and his tension causing involuntary driving aids.

CORRECTION: *Teach the rider, perhaps with the use of the neckstrap, to sit quietly and to go with the pony. Make him aware that he should not give any accidental or unnecessary driving aids.*

PROBLEM (b): The rider habitually shortens his reins just before starting the approach. This becomes a signal to the pony who accelerates while the rider is still sorting out his reins.

CORRECTION: *The rider should, if necessary, adjust his reins in good time before turning on to the approach.*

2. Impetuous pony rushing his fences regardless of the rider's aids

PROBLEM: Poor training or fear.

CORRECTION: *(1) The rider should trot the pony in a circle in front of the fence.*
(2) He should stroke the pony with his outside hand, the outside of his fingers moving up and down the pony's neck, without changing the position of his hand on the rein, or his weight in the saddle. This will help to relieve tension.
(3) He should continue circling until the pony is trotting quietly and rhythmically gradually edging the circle closer to the fence.
(4) He should come quietly off the circle without changing his balance, and then jump the fence.
(5) This should be repeated at several other fences which are well within the pony's capabilities. Impetuous ponies jump best from short approaches and going away from home or from the gate.

3. The pony decelerating and losing impulsion just before take-off

PROBLEM (a): The pony—who may be lacking in confidence or lazy—shifts the insecure rider forward into a position where he is unable to correct him. The pony may then refuse, run out, or jump badly.

CORRECTION: *Teach the rider to maintain the pace of the*
approach, particularly in the last few strides,
when he may have to drive the pony forward
firmly with his legs. If necessary the leg aid may
be reinforced by the whip, used behind the leg.

PROBLEM (b):   The rider approaching from too far away.

CORRECTION: *Let him walk his pony towards the fence from*
about 14 m., breaking into a trot and finally
into a canter for 3 or 4 strides. This helps the
rider to control the approach and to keep the
pony's hocks engaged.

4. The rider looking down and concentrating on the bottom of a fence or ditch *(which often causes refusals or poor jumping)*

PROBLEM: Apprehension or bad habit.

CORRECTION: *Ask a dismounted assistant to stand on the*
landing side of the fence and to hold up a
hand as the rider approaches the fence.
Tell the rider to ride forward with determination,
to look up, and to call out how many fingers the
assistant is showing.

5. The rider unbalancing the pony during the approach

Any sudden or untactful alterations in the rider's balance or contact during a good approach will cause the pony to lose concentration, and will upset his rhythm and balance, thereby spoiling the jump.

PROBLEM (a):   Insecure position.

CORRECTION: *Guidance in improving the position and*
practising the approach will eventually help the
situation. Immediate improvement can be
made by use of the neckstrap.

PROBLEM (b):   Rider swinging forward, the reins becoming
loose in anticipation of the take-off. This causes
the pony to become unbalanced on to his forehand, from where it is difficult for him to jump.

CORRECTION: *Use the neckstrap to give the rider more confi-*
dence so that he will not make any alterations in
his balance or contact just before the take-off.

PROBLEM (c):   Rider habitually interfering with the pony's
stride and rhythm during the approach.

CORRECTION: *Take the fence away, and let the rider practise*
maintaining a correct pace between the wings

PROBLEM (d):
of the fence. Then, as he continues cantering on the circle, build the fence. The rider will then find out how much easier it is for his pony to jump when concentration is not interrupted.
Continuous steady pulling on the reins by the rider during the approach, usually caused by anticipation, and which develops into a habit. The pony, feeling the continuous drag on his mouth, often pulls back. Leaning hard on the rider's hands, he then drops his weight on to the forehand, which makes taking off difficult.

CORRECTION:
Let the rider practise jumping over a combination, either in a jumping lane or alongside a hedge or wall, without holding the reins. (When jumping without reins the ride should be in an enclosed area.) This improves the rider's balance and confidence. He soon learns that he and his pony perform better when they are not having a tug-of-war. Alternatively a neckstrap should be used.

6. The pony running out

The rider loses control in the approach and is unable to hold the pony straight when he dives quickly to one side of the fence.

PROBLEM:
The rider's legs and hands are not effective enough to hold the determined pony straight (Fig. 25a).

CORRECTION:
(1) The rider should turn the pony in the opposite direction to that in which he ran out.
(2) Make sure that the whip is carried at the side on which the pony ran out.
(3) The pony should be walked towards the centre of the fence at an angle of 45 degrees from the side on which he ran out, breaking into trot and finally into canter.
(4) The pony will swing in the same direction as before, will find himself square with the fence, and will jump it. (Fig. 25b).
(5) If the approach is kept at a slow pace the pony will be less likely to get out of control.

The final cure is obviously for the rider to improve the effectiveness of his legs and hands in holding the pony straight.

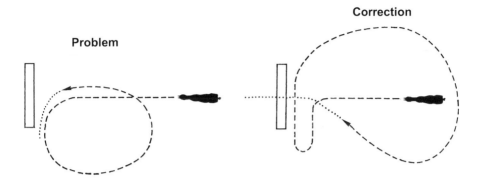

Fig. 25a The wrong track to take when a pony runs out to the left.

Fig. 25b The right track to take when a pony runs out to the left.

Common Problems During the Jump

1. The rider loses balance in front of or behind the movement

PROBLEM (a):   In front of the movement. The rider leans forward abruptly, anticipating the take-off. This unbalances the pony on to his forehand and causes him to take an extra rebalancing stride before taking off. The rider is then unbalanced during the jump.

PROBLEM (b):   Getting left behind. The rider expects the pony to take another stride, and sometimes sits stiffly upright with tight reins, trying to shorten the strides. The pony reacts to this inadvertently given driving aid through the rider's seat, and takes off a stride early. The rider gets left behind and unless he slips the reins, jabs the pony in the mouth.

CORRECTIONS TO BOTH: Use a series of small fences alongside a hedge or wall. With less need to control the pony, the rider can concentrate on feeling the movement of the pony and improving his position. He will also learn to feel the difference in the movement of the take-off stride. If he is in balance and secure at all times, he will be able to retain his position wherever the pony takes off.

Slipping the Reins

More competent riders should be shown how to slip the reins and collect them again. In an emergency, when more rein is needed by the pony than the rider is able to give at that moment, the rider should open his fingers and allow the reins to slip through. He should collect them up again as soon as possible after landing by taking the buckle with one hand and pulling the reins back through the fingers of the other hand, which should remain in the correct. This can be practised:

(a) At the halt and then at the walk, making the change between loose rein walk and medium walk.

(b) With the rider sitting on a chair, his eyes closed, holding the reins as if riding. The Coach/Instructor takes the bit-ends of the reins and moves them from or towards the rider, whose hands must follow. When the reins are suddenly pulled away—as they would be if the rider were to be left behind or if the pony stumbled on landing—the rider must slip the reins.

2. The rider fixes his hands or pulls on the reins

If the rider's hands do not follow the movement of the pony's head and neck, either during take-off or throughout the whole of the jump, the pony will be forced to flatten or hollow his back.

PROBLEM (a):	Rider holding on by the reins because he has not yet developed a secure position.
CORRECTION:	*A neckstrap should be used.*
PROBLEM (b):	Rider has developed a bad habit—such as keeping his hands locked into his stomach or pulling the pony in the mouth during the take-off.
CORRECTION:	*Use jumping lanes or small fences alongside a hedge or wall, the rider practising without holding the reins and with his arms crossed.*
OR	*Sit the rider on a chair, as suggested above for 'Slipping the Reins' but use smooth movements so that the rider learns to follow the movement of the pony's head and neck with his hands.*

3. The rider adopts incorrect leg positions

If the rider stands up in the stirrups or tips on to his knees with his lower legs swinging back and up, the pony will consequently be unbalanced during the jump.

PROBLEM:	Rider not folding forward from his hips. This is due to:
	• Apprehension, which causes tension.
	• The mistaken idea that radical movements will make the pony jump higher.

CORRECTION:	*The rider should practise swinging forward from the hips while riding on the flat. He should then practise jumping doubles or gymnastic jumps, which do not allow time for incorrect movements.*

4. The rider fails to keep his body straight

PROBLEM:	The rider swings his weight to one side and looks down the pony's shoulder, which unbalances the pony.
CORRECTION:	*First check that the rider is sitting square and straight while riding on the flat. Provide something on the landing side which the rider must watch as he jumps, so that he will look forward and straight between his pony's ears. (See correction 4 on page 61).*

Common Problems on Landing

1. The rider's body collapses forward

PROBLEM:	The rider does not absorb through his knees and ankles the change in the direction of the movement.
CORRECTION:	*Physical exercises on the flat, to reduce tension in the joints, will help. The rider should practise standing up in his stirrups with knees and ankles relaxed and as low as possible. Tell him to try to feel this relaxation as the pony lands. Then, if possible, work through a combination of small fences to practise the feel of absorbing the shock of landing over consecutive obstacles.*

2. The rider rounds his back and flops on to the pony's loins

The pony lands, stops as the rider flops on to the back of the saddle, and has difficulty in rebalancing and moving forward.

PROBLEM (a):	The stirrup leathers are too long.
PROBLEM (b):	The lower leg is not secure.
PROBLEM (c):	The rider is tired and loses concentration.
CORRECTION:	*Check the length of the stirrup leathers. Then let the rider trot up to the fence, jump it, and canter away from it. Alternatively, use a double, which will make the rider stay in balance to jump the second element correctly.*

Other Common Problems

Lack of Confidence

The building of confidence should always be in the forefront of the Coach/Instructor's mind. Confidence may be lost by:

(1) A fall. Riders who have a fall as a result of carrying out the Coach/ Instructor's orders will quickly lose confidence in themselves and in the Coach/Instructor.

(2) A bad jump which causes pain to the pony and/or the rider.

(3) Natural timidity.

The situation sometimes becomes worse as pony and rider convince each other of their lack of ability to jump even the smallest obstacle.

CORRECTION: (a) *Make the fences very easy.*

(b) *Use a reliable member of the ride to give a lead.*

(c) *The rider who has problems should hold the neckstrap.*

(d) *With more experienced riders, try the exercise 'Gymnastics without Trotting-Poles', page 121.*

HAZARDS TO AVOID

Do not allow the ride to lose confidence through the following:

• Overfacing. If a fence proves to be too difficult for a pony or rider at their particular stage of training it must be reduced in its dimensions, and confidence must be regained by jumping the smaller fence.

• Slippery going. Rain after a long period of dry weather causes slippery going, which may unbalance ponies and affect their confidence. Choose approach and landing areas with care and reduce the size of fences.

• Wrong distances. When using a double make sure that the distance is satisfactory for the ponies in the ride before making the fences more difficult or before adding a third.

Pain

No pony will jump correctly if he is in pain. Be particularly aware of any signs of lameness, sore backs, or sore mouths. Pain may be the cause of reluctance to move forward or anxiety to complete the jump as quickly as possible. Note that though pain causes tension, tense ponies are not always in pain.

If a pony who normally performs well starts to refuse, he should be examined carefully for any illness or injury which may be causing pain. Ponies which are obviously in pain should not be allowed to jump. Help should be given if possible. Otherwise, veterinary advice should be sought.

11 Jumping Exercises Needing a Small Amount of Equipment

At rallies, the ideal amount of fence building material is seldom available to every ride. The following exercises show some ways in which useful jumping lessons can be given—even to advanced rides— using the minimum amount of equipment. When poles and stands are scarce, it is usually better to build one substantial fence than two flimsy ones.

1. Jumping from a Trot

This is an essential part of the jumping lesson and may be performed with or without the help of trotting-poles. Senior rides will benefit from the use of trotting-poles as long as the horses in the ride have strides of a similar length, and the equipment is available to make at least four trotting-poles and one fence. *See* 'Trotting-Poles and Gymnastic Jumping Exercises', page 116.

   Alternatively, teach the ride to approach a single fence in a steady, rhythmical, rising trot. One or two strides of canter before and after the fence may be permitted. Jumping from the trot is important because:

(a) It is a useful limbering-up exercise, allowing the ponies to stretch their muscles without becoming excited,

(b) It teaches the ponies to jump off their hocks.

(c) A balanced approach in trot is the forerunner of a balanced approach in canter. It is therefore a stage in teaching a young or unbalanced pony to jump correctly.

(d) It gives riders and ponies confidence to know that they can jump competently at a slow pace. This is particularly important on a cross-country course, where some fences may have to be tackled slowly.

(e) Jumping from trot then cantering on landing is a useful exercise, especially for those who ride up to a fence but stop riding forward at the last moment, causing their ponies to stop or just struggle over.

2. Jumping Off a Circle

If the ride is capable of achieving a reasonable 30 m. circle in canter, a useful exercise may be performed by including a fence on the circle.

(a) In turn, each rider canters a circle, leaving the fence on the outside, until the rhythm, energy, and balance are correct.

(b) Without losing the bend, he enlarges the circle slightly to include the fence, continuing afterwards on the circle without changing the pace. Most members will make three circles, jumping the fence on the second circuit. If a pony rushes at the fence, or otherwise breaks the rhythm of the canter, the rider should turn inside the fence until the rhythm is reestablished.

(c) The exercise should be carried out on both reins. If space is limited, use the same circle and a fence which is jumpable from both directions, such as a 'hog's back'.

If the riders are advanced enough to work independently several members may perform at once, each with their own fence. However, each rider will jump only when commanded by the Coach/Instructor who will then watch that particular individual. The others will continue to canter in circles until they, in turn, are told to jump. The circles should not overlap. Beware of keeping any pony cantering for too long.

3. Doubles

Simple doubles at correct distances promote rhythm and balance.
They teach the rider to:
(a) Maintain position.
(b) Ride forward.
(c) Ride straight to the centre of the second element.

Equipment Required:

A minimum of two pairs of stands and four poles.

- After some preliminary movements and jumping the ride over a single fence, build a double with 10 m. (approx. 33 ft.) between the two fences. Keep the fences small until you are sure that the distance is satisfactory.
- It is most unlikely that the ponies in a ride will have strides of identical length. It will, therefore, be impossible to build a double which is perfect for the whole ride. If the average height is 14 hh., the free-moving ponies will take two non-jumping strides, and those with shorter strides will have room to make three, without breaking their rhythm.
- If the double is on a gradient, the distance will need to be slightly shorter when approached uphill, and longer when going downhill.
- Use the fence from both directions, but remember to change the ground-lines.
- A one non-jumping stride double may be built if the ponies have similar lengths of stride.
- Start with the fence at 6.25 m. (approx. 20.5 ft.) apart but be prepared to adjust the distance so that the ponies jump it easily in their stride. Those with more ability may need 7.25 m. (almost 24 ft.).

4. Cross-Poles

These encourage the ride to make a habit of jumping in the centre of their fences. Fences may be made more challenging by adjusting the angle and the height in the centre. They are useful as a training aid and fun for all

rides to jump. Having jumped them successfully from a normal approach, more advanced rides may have the fences as the centre of a figure-of-eight, in trot or canter.
- The ride should first achieve acceptable circles in trot and canter on both reins.
- Each rider in turn may then practise a figure-of-eight, first in trot and then in canter, without the poles in place, changing the leg through trot between the jump stands.
- Then try it with the cross-poles in place.
- The ponies will generally land with the other leg leading.
- Unless the ponies have been well schooled, these exercises will prove hard.
- Two or three lessons may be needed because an acceptable standard must be reached at each stage before progressing to the next.
- The exercise is valuable because it teaches the riders to:
  (a) Ride circles.
  (b) Straighten their ponies.
  (c) Develop the opposite bend.

5. Counting Strides

Middle rides enjoy an exercise which includes counting *'One, two, three, jump'* during the last few strides of the approach, which in this case should be straight and in canter. The exercise is helpful in teaching judgement of distances and lengths of strides, By calling *'jump'* on the take-off stride, the rider will learn the difference in feel between it and the non-jumping strides. Counting strides also helps to maintain a constant rhythm and prevents the rider from holding his breath.
Procedure:
- Ensure that the ride is performing fluently over the fence.
- Tell the riders to call 'jump' during the take-off stride.
- Make them count the last few strides.
- The riders should not interfere with their ponies in order to make their counting correct.

6. Gradients

If there is a hollow or a hill in the field, the ride may be taught how to compensate for the gradient, when jumping uphill and down. The fence should be low and fixed securely. A pole rolling downhill can cause an accident. Logs firmly wedged on both sides with small stakes are ideal. A wedged pole on the ground is a useful starter. Jump the ride uphill first. Some ponies may buck or run away downhill, until they have expended some energy.

Going uphill, more energy will be needed. The ponies should, and generally will, take off nearer than usual to the fence, because the higher up the hill they get before taking off, the lower the fence will be. They should not be allowed to sprawl up the hill with their hocks out behind, as their hocks must be well engaged when they arrive at the place where they will take off.

Going downhill, balance should be maintained and speed should be controlled. Less advanced rides should start downhill very slowly, to discourage their ponies from taking huge leaps and landing at the bottom. More advanced rides will do this by controlling the pace and keeping the length of stride short.

7. Ditches
These are not ideal obstacles for beginners, but they sometimes need to be negotiated in the course of cross-country rides or while moving from one area to another at camp.
- Ponies sometimes jump big over ditches, so inexperienced riders should hold on to neckstraps.
- As no poles are involved, the ride may follow on at the walk with 3 or 4 lengths between each pony.
- A bold pony should be leading file.
- The riders should look forward into the next field. They should never look down into the bottom of the ditch.
- It helps if the ditch is first jumped towards home.
- Ponies are less apprehensive of natural, as opposed to artificial, ditches.
- It is not advisable for the Coach/Instructor to lead the pony over, as ponies sometimes jump into those leading them.
- It may be possible to lead the pony down an easier place into the ditch, along it, and up the other side.
- If a pony persistently refuses, seek advice from a senior Coach/Instructor.

8. Jumping from Different Angles over Different Parts of the Fence
Young horses and less experienced riders should be taught to jump in the centre of their fences but, as training progresses, rides should be taught to vary the line of approach. Use one fence, two pieces of ribbon, and four markers. Cones are ideal, but logs, or plastic buckets with their handles removed, are an acceptable substitute. Tie the ribbons round the top pole of the fence one-third and two thirds along.

(a) After some preliminary exercises, during which the fence is jumped straight and the ride is assessed, ask each rider to describe a correct arc and to jump the fence between the ribbon and the upright (Fig. 26, line A). As always, insist that the ride works towards producing a smooth, balanced, rhythmical movement.

(b) If the ride proves that it can jump anywhere along the pole, and accurately over a ribbon, on a straight line, tell the riders to try jumping off a large circle, about 30 m. in diameter, inside the buckets and over the fence (line B).

(c) Practise jumping the fence, between the ribbons, at an angle on a straight line from the inside of one marker to the inside of the diagonal marker (line C). Note that though this line may appear to be straight when approaching to jump from left to right, the rider will have the pony bent slightly to the left. After the fence the pony will be bent to the right. Note that in Fig. 26 no arrows are shown, as each exercise may be performed either way. Remember to change the ground lines.

These exercises can vary from simple to complicated, depending on the standard of the ride.

• Junior rides may perform them at a walk, with ribbons on the pole on the ground.

• Middle rides enjoy team games, with top marks scored by those who can describe a correct arc and jump a low fence over a ribbon.

SHOULD PROBLEMS ARISE, ALWAYS REVERT TO A STRAIGHT APPROACH TO THE CENTRE OF THE FENCE.

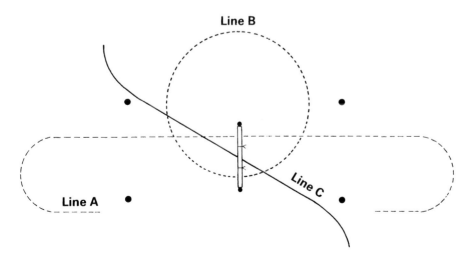

Fig. 26 Jumping from different angles over different parts of the fence.

9. Jumping from Slow and Fast Speeds

Advanced rides may need to practise jumping at different speeds off different lengths of stride. The two extremes may be practised, using in each case a single fence. Suitable exercises are:

(a) Jumping Off a Short Stride in Canter

Use an upright fence which looks solid but will knock down. The strides should be full of impulsion and the rhythm active, although the speed is slow and the strides are short. This should be maintained through the whole movement.

- Reduce the length of approach to a minimum. The object is to teach the rider how to cope with short approaches, such as jumping out of country lanes when hunting. Also, ponies often become frustrated cantering slowly on a long approach.
- Put a marker a few strides from the fence.
- Each rider should approach the marker at the correct pace, at a right-angle to the fence. Then he should turn inside the marker and jump the fence.
- A correct bend is essential.
- The exercise should be carried out on both reins.
- After the ride has completed the exercise successfully, quick turns may be practised on the landing side to simulate jumping into a lane.
- Following this demanding exercise, work the ride over a large staircase fence, off a normal stride, to reestablish free forward movement.

(b) Jumping from the Gallop

This should be taught only by senior Coach/Instructors who will first ensure that exercises using a normal schooling fence have been completed satisfactorily, and that a well-built steeplechase fence—which leans away from the take-off—is available.

Teach the ride to gallop at a balanced, rhythmical pace, using the correct galloping position, before attempting to jump. Horses will find their own strides at the gallop as long as they are allowed to concentrate during the approach. Riders should therefore sit still, keeping an even contact but ready to react immediately to any variation in the pace.

Jumping from the gallop should be the last exercise of the lesson.

Leave time for the horses to warm down.

Taking the Dismounted Ride

12 Instruction in Horse and Pony Care

Riders must understand that horsemastership in all its aspects is of vital importance. Without good care, no pony, however talented, and well ridden will ever achieve his full potential. Ignorance can lead to suffering and can cause lasting damage. Because horsemastership does not come naturally and requires mental effort and application, it must be taught in an interesting way.

The Dismounted Group Lesson

By far the most satisfactory way of teaching care is by giving practical lessons, using either members' own ponies and equipment or, if it is a dismounted rally, some pre-planned facilities.

Preparation

Find out:

(a) **The ride:** what are the ages, standards, and number of riders in the group?

(b) **Facilities:** where will the lesson be held? What props are available?

(c) **Time:** how long will the lesson will be?

(d) **Subject:** the Chief Coach/Instructor will tell you the subject (e.g. clipping or feeding) to be taught. Otherwise, make your own decision according to (a), (b), and (c) above.

Read: the relevant parts of the current *Manual of Horsemanship* and take notes of the main points.

Choose those aspects which apply to the standard and age of the ride.

Plan how you will give an entertaining talk and demonstration. These should, as a rule, take one-quarter of the lesson time, leaving three-quarters in which the ride can practise.

Coaches/Instructors should insist on high standards of practical work from the ride, as this will increase interest and pride in the results.

NOTE: Be aware of weather conditions. The riders will not pay attention if they are too cold or too wet or too hot.

The following sample lesson on the subject of grooming is explained in detail to show how this type of lesson should be prepared and taught. A good way of revising is to have each member in turn acting as coach and demonstrator for the various phases.

Grooming

This sample lesson is suitable for any riders aged 6 to 12 who keep their ponies stabled or at grass. It can take place at a day rally or on the first day of camp after a mounted lesson. Each member should have a headcollar with rope, and a complete grooming kit. If the ponies are to be turned out at night, avoid grooming their backs too thoroughly as this removes the protective natural grease.

Before the Lesson

Choose a safe place for the ponies to be tied up, e.g. along a fence in a field, or in an enclosed yard. Decide (a) which pony and grooming kit you will borrow for your demonstration, (b) where you will tie the pony, (c) where you will lay out the grooming kit and (d) where the class will sit, so that everyone can watch and hear you easily.

Taking the Lesson

After seeing that the ponies are unsaddled and tied up correctly, lay out the grooming kit on a table or straw bale and begin your lesson.
You should deal with:

1. **The reasons for grooming:** involve the group by asking questions.
2. **How to prepare for grooming:** check how the pony to be used for the demonstration is tied up. Take off hats and coats and put them in a clean, safe place. If it is warm, roll up sleeves.
3. **The names and uses of each item of grooming kit:** ask the group to tell you the names of the items. Demonstrate the correct use of each item by grooming one side of the pony, but be sure to point out that in reality both sides should be groomed!
4. **Practice:** each member should groom their own pony while you watch and correct faults. The pony which you have used for demonstrating will have the other side groomed by his rider. Remember that very young members will need help.

At the end of the period take a few minutes (a) to ask a few questions to satisfy yourself that the main points have been absorbed, and (b) to answer any other questions that the ride may have.

Other Subjects (Using Lesson Plan for Grooming)

Subjects which could be prepared and taught in similar fashion to grooming are bandaging, clipping and trimming, first aid and surgical bandaging, mucking out, plaiting, mane pulling, and tack-cleaning.

Shoeing

'No foot—no horse' is an oft-repeated and wise saying. All members should learn the basic facts about the care of a pony's feet and shoeing, but it is important that they should not go away from a shoeing lesson thinking that they know enough to be critical of a trained farrier's work. If they are genuinely worried about the way in which their pony is being shod, they should seek advice from a knowledgeable person. In time they will have had enough experience to make their own judgement.

To Be Taught Before 'B' Test (15 to 16 years)

(a) Reasons for shoeing (which should include knowledge of the external points of the foot).
(b) How to tell that a pony needs shoeing.
(c) The difference between hot and cold shoeing.
(d) The farrier's tools—their names and functions.
(e) What the farrier has to do: - to remove an old shoe.
           - to prepare the foot.
           - to prepare and fit the new shoe.
           - to nail on and finish off.
(f) How to tell whether a pony has been well shod.
(g) Various types of common shoes, the names of their parts; nails and studs.
(h) The structure of a pony's foot—the names and functions of the various parts.

Allow 45-minute periods for the lessons below.

Preliminary Lessons: (a) Reasons for shoeing.
        (b) How to tell that a pony needs shoeing.
        (c) Preparation of the feet, explaining how this relates to (d) below.
        (d) How to tell whether a pony has been well-shod.

Requirements:
• A healthy, well cared for foot.
• An overgrown hoof with a too long and turned-up toe (which illustrates the importance of farriers' visits to ponies at grass).
• One or more ponies with risen clenches and loose or thin shoes.
• A large drawing or diagram of a badly-shod foot and another of a wellshod foot.

Follow-Up Lessons

There is still too much to be taught and too much information to be absorbed for one 45-minute period. Therefore plan two follow-up lessons and a practical demonstration if possible.

Lesson 1: (a) Revision of preliminary lesson.
(b) Hot and cold shoeing—advantages and disadvantages.
(c) Structure of a pony's foot.
(d) Varieties of common shoes—nails and studs.

Requirements:
• A specimen of a horse's or a pony's hoof and bones, from the fetlock down. A chart showing a pony's lower leg and hoof.
• A variety of common shoes both fore and hind. Nails and studs.

Lesson 2: (a) Revision of previous lessons.
(b) Farrier's tools and their uses.
(c) Removal of an old shoe, then preparing, fitting, and nailing on a shoe.

Requirements:
• A set of farrier's tools in their box.
• A quiet horse for a mock shoeing.

Practical Demonstration

A visit to a forge or—better still, as forges are not designed for class instruction—a visit to a rally or camp by a farrier with a mobile forge. Demonstrations by craftsmen require careful arranging beforehand, so that the group will gain maximum benefit. It is advisable to deal with part of the subject, (a) and (b) above before the demonstration, rather than afterwards.

Some farriers are able to explain their work clearly. Others may need help to supplement their commentary. Some may agree to shoe each hoof individually; in this case arrange for a small group to watch one hoof being shod and then change over to another group for the next hoof, rather than having everyone watching at the same time.

Requirements:
• A farrier with his forge and tools.
• A supply of water for his bucket.
• One pony to be shod.
• If visiting the forge, transport for members of the group.

The Five-Minute Talk

During the course of a rally the Coach/Instructor might decide that the ponies in his or her group were particularly suitable for teaching a certain topic; or might have noticed that a certain aspect of stable management was generally sub-standard. Using a break in the mounted lesson, or after lunch, he or she might take the opportunity to discuss the subject with the riders, using their ponies and equipment. He or she should give sympathetic help and advice where necessary, and should point out something correct or good about every pony, leaving everyone wiser, and no one demoralised.

Subjects might be:

- Types of girths.
- Fitting of nosebands (particularly drop and flash nosebands).
- Fitting a snaffle bit.
- Use of numnahs.
- Indication for re-shoeing.
- Colours or markings.

Or with older rides:

- Fitting curb chains.
- Types of saddles.
- Respiratory problems.

Although this is no substitute for a class lesson, it is a useful way of pointing out to the group a common weakness or something unusual which would be of interest to them, such as an Appaloosa pony (juniors), a pony shod with rolled toe shoes (middle ride) or a spavin (seniors).

Horse Care Tasks

This is a way of teaching large numbers at a dismounted rally and is described on page 20 in Chapter 2.

13 Giving a Lecture

Lectures are used for teaching theoretical subjects such as the principles of feeding and conditioning. Because the subjects will be academic rather than practical, there will be few props, and the Coach/Instructor must rely on charts and diagrams to illustrate the talk. To prevent boredom, involve the audience with small tasks and questions. Word searches or quizzes may enliven the subject.

Study your subject so that you can speak with confidence. Use knowledge acquired from your own experience, from other people, and from books. Know all the different aspects of the subject so that you can discuss it from various angles.

Plan a lecture of the appropriate length, presented in a logical sequence, as this makes it easier to understand and remember. Be clear and simple.

Prepare notes which can be abbreviated and written on postcards in clearly set out headings, but have the detail in your mind. Lectures which are read straight from books or scripts can be boring.

Memorise your opening and closing sentences.

Use some visual aids according to the type of lecture, the venue, and the size of the audience. 'The eye is the window to the brain'.

For example:

(a) Samples of bones, feeds, saddlery or other 'real' items to illustrate your talk. But pass them round only at appropriate times, or they may be distracting.

(b) Diagrams prepared in advance.

(c) Flip chart and pens or blackboard and chalks.

(d) Viewing aids such as overhead projectors, smart boards or PowerPoint, etc, are useful, and are often at hand if you are lecturing at a school. With an overhead projector, you can make drawings on transparencies either before or during the lecture. One transparency may be placed above another: for example, the outline of a pony may be saddled up or rugged-up.

Whenever possible, *demonstrate* how something should be done. Young members especially like to *watch* something at times during the lecture.

Points to Remember

- Know your subject and prepare it adequately. Most lecturers feel apprehensive before they start; nerves will disappear once you begin.
- Speak slowly and clearly, look at your audience, and ensure that people in the back row can hear.
- Try to avoid mannerisms, which can be distracting.
- Speak with conviction.
- Make their minds work by asking questions during your lecture.
- Leave some time at the end to answer questions, and ask some yourself to bring out specific points.
- Summarise your lecture and offer a conclusion.
- Ask questions so you can ascertain learning has taken place.

14 Using Audio Visual Equipment

The use of video or DVD, both for viewing prerecorded material and for making recordings, is of great value.

Requirements

For Viewing   A television set or computer.
                         Power source.
                         A video/DVD player.

For Filming   A video camera—preferably with tripod.

If you have a video camera with a TV playback facility you will be able to review your own recorded material immediately.

The Video/DVD Player

One of the great advantages is that the Coach/Instructor can take total control of the programme and repeat any section as many times as necessary. Other advantages are:
• Fast rewind.
• Slow motion.
• Static picture.

Important Note

Before buying or hiring information or teaching tapes or DVDs, check that their contents are compatible with Pony Club and British Horse Society teaching methods.

   Preparation is essential. Before showing videos, play them through, and decide how to use them. This takes longer than you think!

Suggested Uses

• At a dismounted rally with 10 to 12 members of approximately the same age and standard. This is a useful way of including members who do not have their own ponies.
• At a mounted rally or at camp, with the video equipment set up in a horsebox or building, where groups can come in at prearranged times with their Coach/Instructors.
• As a quiz, with questions compiled in advance.

The Video Camera

The video camera can be a most useful addition to any lesson. There are many ways in which it can be used—to improve riding ability, increase knowledge, develop awareness and provide fun.

To gain most benefit from it:
- The activity filmed must be compatible with the standard of the ride.
- Work in small groups.
- The Coach/Instructor should not be the camera operator.
- The Coach/Instructor should explain to the operator exactly what he or she hopes to achieve with the lesson, and whether side, front or back views are required.
- The Coach/Instructor should stand near to the operator so that all his or her comments will be picked up on the recorder.
- If any unfortunate incidents should occur which the Coach/Instructor would like to have erased the operator must be asked to do this before continuing filming.
- Viewing of the film should be arranged as soon as possible after the lesson that it shows.

Warnings

- Remember that young children are very excited when they see their pony on the screen for the first time. Several replays may be required before they settle down and attend to the lesson.
- Be particularly aware that older, more mature, members are often shocked and demoralised when they see a recording. The image that they have of themselves and their ponies may be very different from what actually appears on the screen. The camera must serve the same purpose as good instruction—and be CONSTRUCTIVE.

Suggestions for Filming

1. A Jumping Lesson (for All Rides)

The ride should be filmed while jumping, from the side and the rear. The filming should continue while the Coach/Instructor makes comments to each rider after their turn, pointing out their faults and suggesting how these should be corrected. The lesson should then continue (without filming) until the Coach/Instructor is satisfied that every rider shows at least some improvement. Finally the ride can be re-filmed jumping, as before. The ride should be shown the film as soon as possible. Each member will then learn, by seeing their own improvement, by listening to the Coach/ Instructor's comments and by watching the efforts of the other members of the ride. Thus the lesson will be confirmed in a most positive way.

2. A Movement to Ride (for More-Experienced Members)

Once riders have become accustomed to the camera and to their appearance on the screen, the Coach/Instructor can use his or her ingenuity and devise ways of helping them to relate what they feel to what they finally see. While the camera is recording, encourage them to talk about 'how their horse is going'. This helps them to analyse what they have felt and to express themselves clearly. When watching the film they may also check that their comments were relevant.

3. Horse and Pony Care

As an aid to teaching stable management, each ride at camp could prepare a demonstration on pony care. These could then be filmed, and a useful teaching tape made—fun and learning combined.

4. Other Suggestions

Branch competitions can be filmed, and shown at a fund-raising evening held for parents and friends. The branch can make its own demonstration tapes, with more senior members responsible for the organising. Road safety and countryside studies are among suitable topics.

Further Subjects for Instruction

15 Countryside Studies and Hunting

An understanding of Countryside Studies and Hunting should be taught in all branches, regardless of whether or not The Pony Club Achievement Badges Scheme is used. Teaching should be according to local conditions and by knowledgeable local people (who need not be riding instructors). Occasionally the Coach/Instructor and a farmer, or an expert in some aspect of countryside studies, might take the lesson together. The 'expert' can give the main lesson, and the Coach/Instructor can join in a general discussion or question session, so that the ride learns the subject from different points of view. Such lessons are best given during country rides, when observations can be made at first hand.

Members who hunt should have some knowledge of countryside studies. The importance of teaching courteous behaviour and responsible riding cannot be over-stressed.

Ways of Teaching Countryside Studies

1. On instructional hacks (country rides), perhaps in an afternoon at a day rally (*see* Chapter 2, page 16).
2. On a farm walk, perhaps on a summer evening, followed by a barbecue.
3. During dismounted rallies held at farms, when groups might be taken for a guided tour either on foot or on an open trailer behind a tractor.
4. At lectures, or walks in natural surroundings, under the guidance of experts.
5. As members of a BHS bridlepath working party.

Depending on local conditions, suitable subjects might be:

(a) **Farming:** how and when it is possible to ride through farmland without causing any damage. Recognising crops, spring and autumn cultivations. Recognising stock and its condition. Maintenance of land; drainage, the dangers of sub-soiling and mole draining to riders. Types of fencing and use of gates. Provision of water for stock.

(b) **Bridle Paths:** how to use them without inconveniencing any other users. The law relating to them.

(c) **Forestry:** rules to observe when riding through woods. Maintenance of trees and paths. Recognising young trees. Fire precautions.

(d) **Fishing and Shooting:** riding without disturbing game or annoying fishermen. Preservation of game. Rearing seasons. Sporting rights, shooting syndicates, fishing clubs.

(e) **Natural History:** recognising and being able to name the flora and fauna of the countryside. The characteristics of the seasons.

Hunting

Hunting conditions vary in different areas, but all members should realise that we hunt by courtesy of landowners and farmers, and that good manners towards all concerned, and particularly the general public, are essential.

Ways of Teaching Hunting

1. Through practical experience, starting with children's or Pony Club meets, and following the Hunting Test Certificate.
2. At mock hunts. (*See* Chapter 2, page 17).
3. With lectures, which may include a demonstration of the use of the horn.
4. With videos of hunting which have well-informed commentaries.
5. With lectures or discussions during rallies.
6. With visits to kennels.

Subjects might include:

(a) **The Fox:** his lifestyle.
(b) **The Hunt:** its Masters, administration, kennels, hunt servants, supporters.
(c) **Hounds:** breeding, rearing, walking, entering, exercising, hunting.
(d) **Use of the Hunting Whip:** cracking it; opening gates; warning hounds away from ponies' heels.
(e) **Preparations:** fitness of pony. Finding out venue of meet and cost of subscription or cap. Sensible choice of saddlery and clothing. Contents of pockets—money, string, penknife, snacks, etc.
(f) **The Meet:** how to behave, who to identify, who to pay.
(g) **Hunting Language:** expressions used. The horn. Hound language.
(h) **The Hunting Day:** description of particularly interesting hunts which have taken place locally. Imagining situations which might occur concerning hounds, hunt servants, field master, the field. Behaviour in the field.
(i) **The End of the Day:** etiquette when leaving the field. Riding home. Consideration for pony.

16 Road Safety

All road safety training is done OFF the public roads and is progressive. There are three tests and details can be found on the Pony Club website. The tests are as follows:

1. Road Rider Mini Achievement Badge to be taken at E to D Test level.
2. Road Rider Achievement Badge to be taken at D+ to C Test level.
3. Road Rider Test to be taken at C+ to B Test level.

Early Training

Training must begin at the first opportunity. On enrolment new members should purchase the *Junior Road Rider* book, and the *Road Rider* DVD. Early rallies should include some instruction on the subject. Every effort should be made to alert parents to the dangers of their children riding on the road. This can be done in a number of ways:

• At parents' meetings, where DVDs can be shown.
• Involving parents in teaching the *Highway Code*.
• At rallies, with parents acting as helpers during simulated road tests.
• At evening quizzes with members.

The Object of the Tests

Riders should be so well schooled in road safety manoeuvres and hand signals that these become automatic, leaving the rider free to cope with the pony in traffic or in other difficult situations.

Planning Instruction for the Tests

Mounted

• Know the requirements of the tests. (Study the current Pony Club and British Horse Society publications, the *Road Rider* DVD, and the *Highway Code.*
• Plan a progressive programme of 10 to 15 minute periods, to be fitted into every rally.
  OR
• Plan a series of road safety rallies.

Either method should end with practice of a simulated road test. Remember to organise any special props—cones, traffic signs, material for marking lines and road junctions, hazards, etc. Position them in advance.

Dismounted (Indoors)
A great deal can be achieved during winter rallies or camp, using the following:
• *Road Rider* DVD.
• A talk.
• Magnetic board, blackboard or table model—to facilitate discussion of traffic situations which arise while riding on the road.
• Quiz.

NOTE:
The Road Rider Tests are for the rider, not the pony. Though training involves the pony, it is primarily concerned with the rider. Training should increase the safety of riders on the road, but there can never be any positive guarantee against accidents.

If ponies prove unsuitable to be ridden in the tests, parents should be notified. In such cases, the ponies should neither be used for the test nor ridden on the road.

17 Preparing a Ride for Pony Club Competitions

(a) Riding a Dressage Test
The prospect of a dressage test can be very alarming to many young riders, and Coaches/Instructors can help by building up confidence. You should explain that (1) in its simple form dressage is just ordinary training, aimed at producing an obedient pony who goes in a correct way and who is pleasant to ride, and (2) that a dressage test is designed to assess just how successful that training has been. Before attempting a test, members of the ride should be able to perform all the basic movements required, and should be mounted on reasonably obedient ponies. A half-forgotten test on a disobedient pony can easily end in tears and can lead to a lasting dislike of dressage.
Confidence can be built up by:
• Learning the test so well that the rider can concentrate on the movements.
• Understanding what is required (sometimes outlined in *Directive Ideas* on the test sheet) so that there is a sense of achievement when movements are performed well.

- Realising that one bad movement or error of course is not the end of the world, as each movement is marked separately.
- Practising any movements which may be unfamiliar.
- Knowing the procedure at a dressage competition.

Although this lesson can be useful to the more experienced who need to brush up their arena-craft, it is intended mainly for those who are just starting to do dressage tests.

Before the Mounted Lesson
Learning the Test

Learning something by memory is an individual problem, and the ability to do so varies widely. This puts severe limitations on achieving it in a ride lesson. The Coach/Instructor can help by suggesting aids to memory, and by revising whenever a suitable opportunity presents itself, such as after lunch at a day rally or when sheltering from a sudden downpour of rain.

1. The Coach/Instructor can usefully run through the test on a flip chart to make sure that everyone understands what is required.
2. More lasting value will result if each rider is asked to draw an arena on paper and then to trace in the movements.
3. Junior rides will enjoy practising on foot in an arena (approx. 5 x 10 m.) outlined in chalk on a hard surface.

Checking the Rules

Find out which rules are being used, then instruct the members to read the rule book. Check that they know:

- The saddlery, dress and equipment that may or may not be used for the test and while working-in.
- Whether anyone else is allowed to ride the pony on the day of the competition.
- Any other rules which might cause problems.

The Mounted Lesson
Requirements

(1) A dressage arena accurately laid out with white boards, letters, and corner markers on a flat place where the going is reasonably good. Try to make the arena as impressive as it will look in the competition itself. Park your car close to the arena at 'C', where the judge's car is usually stationed.

(2) An assistant, if there are likely to be more than five members in the ride. You can divide them into two groups. The assistant should be capable of helping a group with basic paces and transitions.

Starting the Lesson

Start with the whole ride, as set out in Chapter 5, 'Procedure' (page 34). During the working-in period, riders and ponies should settle and become accustomed to working close to the white boards and the car. Then line up the ride and *explain* that you are going to teach:

(a) What to do at a dressage competition.

(b) How to use the arena correctly.

Discuss

(a) On which rein each member will ride before making their entry.

(b) How to ride through the corners without upsetting the pony's balance and rhythm.

(c) How to ride accurately, following the movements laid down in the test, and preparing the pony carefully for the transitions and changes in direction. Having been prepared, transitions written in the test should be made as the *rider* reaches the appropriate marker.

Using the maximum distances between the ponies, the ride can then practice:

• Correctly ridden corners.

• Correctly ridden shapes of basic movements in the test, such as circles, changing the rein across the diagonal, or riding on to the centre line.

Discuss

(a) Any unusual movement in the test, if necessary by demonstrating its shape on foot.

(b) Any movements which involve lengthening and shortening the reins, or riding with the reins in one hand.

Again, using maximum distances between ponies, the ride should *practice* the above.

Individual Practice in the Arena

If there are more than five in the ride, take groups of three or four at a time to work in the arena while your assistant helps the others to work on basic paces and transitions near the arena. Divide your time equally between the groups.

Choose your most experienced rider to ride the first movement of the test. He should show:

(a) How to report any changes of pony or rider. This should be to the steward or writer, not to the judge.

(b) How to ride around the outside of the arena until the car-horn or the bell sounds.

(c) A correct turn on to the centre line before entering the arena.

(d) A straight line and a good, still halt.

(e) A correct salute executed without disturbing the pony.

(f) A straight move-off, whether or not a halt is required.

While standing in a ride each member might then practice the salute at the halt. Stress again the importance of preparing the ponies in advance for changes in direction or transitions—always thinking and looking ahead. Your next rider can demonstrate the next few movements, and so on, until the end of the test. The rider performing the final movements should also show how to leave the arena.

Riders who are not performing should watch with you, near to 'C', and be encouraged to observe and make comments to you.

Make corrections at the moment when they are needed. If necessary, revise movements which have caused problems, allowing the riders to perform them again.

To finish, discuss turnout and dress as well as a sensible working-in routine to be used on the day of the competition. This will vary according to the individual characteristics of the pony.

Conclusion

There will seldom be time for all members to ride the whole test individually during the lesson, and they must be encouraged to practise the movements on their own. Warn them that while they may run through the test a few times on their ponies, they must avoid constant repetition, or the ponies will begin to anticipate.

NOTE:

All dressage tests are tests of correct training. Movements performed in Pony Club dressage tests should therefore have been practised at previous Pony Club rallies. The lesson outlined above should consist of revising, practising the movements, and ensuring that every member of the ride has the benefit of working individually, under supervision, in a dressage arena. The use of video can be invaluable if it is presented in a constructive way. (*See* Chapter 14, page 80).

(b) Show Jumping

The Course

A good show-jumping course consists of a mixture of staircase, upright and parallel fences. Enough equipment should be available to build a good flowing course with turns in both directions and including at least one double. The first few fences should be comparatively easy. For junior rides, the first fence should be jumped in the direction of the ride. For junior and middle rides the double should be constructed as two upright fences with 9 to 10 m. (approx. 30 to 33 ft.) between them, depending on the height of the fences and the size of the ponies. For advanced rides, spread fences may be used in doubles or trebles. The distances should be measured from the last element of the first fence to the first element of the second. Only the first fence of a double may be a spread.

When setting the height of the fences, always err on the side of caution. You can easily enlarge them once the ride has proved that they are too easy.

Have the course ready before the lesson begins. For further information on course building see the Pony Club publication *Building Show Jumping Courses* and the British Show Jumping *Notes on Course Building for Show Jumping*.

Assistants

If possible have some dismounted members to help with the fences.

Walking the Course

At competitions, riders must walk the course on foot. At rallies, if the ponies can be left safely it is preferable for the ride to inspect the course on foot. Otherwise 'walk' the course with the ride mounted.

Discuss

(a) The track or path to be taken by each pony, a correct line of approach to every fence.

(b) Any undulations in the ground, and the effect on balance and impulsion.

(c) Any other difficulties, such as spread fences after corners, or doubles and trebles.

(d) The importance of knowing the course so well from start to finish that each rider can concentrate on their riding and their pony without fear of going the wrong way.

Fig. 27 An exercise on the flat.

Preliminary Work on the Flat

After some preliminary exercises, ask each rider to demonstrate the pace in which the course should be jumped. Junior rides should achieve a canter, maintaining the same speed on a circle and a straight line. More advanced rides should achieve an active, balanced, rhythmical canter from which the pony can adjust his stride without breaking his rhythm. The following exercise enables the ride to practise this without jumping the ponies.

Put out six markers as shown in Fig. 27.

Tell each rider to perform a circle of about 20 m., followed by a straight line of about 60 m., followed by another circle the same size as the first, followed by a returning straight line. Working one at a time, the ride could:

1. Practise riding the shape of the exercise in trot.
2. Ride it in canter, keeping a constant rhythm.
3. Proceed as in (2) but count aloud the strides between the markers and ask for some stronger strides on the returning line, which should also be counted. The return will probably be made with one or two fewer strides.
4. As (3) but ask for shorter than normal strides on the returning line. The circles should always be performed at the basic jumping canter, which is active and from which the individual pony can easily lengthen or shorten his stride. The exercise should be carried out on both reins. Some show-jumping ponies shorten their strides by swinging their hindquarters sideways. Their riders should attempt to control the quarters and to ride the ponies straight. Depending on the standard of the ride, the exercise may be varied. Suggest that the ride pretends that there is a large parallel fence halfway down the straight line. This would necessitate asking for stronger strides on the last quarter of the circle so that the pace is established before the mock fence. (Do not mark the exact position, or the riders might spoil the exercise by abruptly trying to 'find a stride'.) Or pretend that there is a large, narrow fence a quarter of the way down the straight line. This would need to be 'jumped' from a short, active canter, which would give the pony time to see the fence and judge his stride ready for take-off.

Jumping the Course in Sections

If a practice fence is available, it may be preferable to work the more advanced ride over it and then over the whole course, as in a competition. With a less experienced ride or a ride of young horses, it helps to jump the course in sections.

Each pony should jump the first fence, which will be small and simple. The rest of the course may be tackled one or two fences at a time. The riders' positions and the methods of approach, jump, and recovery should be corrected if necessary. Sluggish ponies may need leads to get them going. The double may cause problems: make it simple at first, and ensure that timid ponies have a 'carrot' about 20 m. away on the landing side.

Jumping the Whole Course

- Discuss the rules and methods used in judging show jumping.
- Remind the ride of the points discussed and the plans made while walking the course.
- Emphasise the importance of executing the plan accurately (riding the corners correctly, etc.).
- Have a 'start', a 'finish', and a whistle or some signal for the riders to begin. The ride will then become familiar with show jumping procedure.

Next, tell each rider in turn to jump the course. While the course is being jumped, stress the importance of rhythm, balance and speed control throughout the whole round. The rhythm should remain constant. Correct those riders who lose the rhythm on the corners while they take a rest. Although sluggish ponies may have to be ridden hard at their fences, the average pony moving with sufficient impulsion will jump better if he is not pulled almost to a standstill and then suddenly bustled at the fence for the last three strides.

Point out mistakes to the rest of the ride as they occur. After each round discuss how successfully the course was ridden. Did the rider stay on the track as planned? Was he able to maintain rhythm, balance and impulsion? Why were fences knocked down? Did the rider take away the pony's concentration or unbalance him by looking back to see if a pole had fallen at the previous fence? Did the pony run out at the double because the rider failed to ride to the centre of the second (final) element?

The Second Round

Any riders who had difficulty the first time round should jump the same course again—trying, with the Coach/Instructor's help, to correct their mistakes. For those who had little difficulty, the fences may be raised and made wider according to the ability of the ride.

The Timed Jump-off

Use a shortened course with turns both ways. Explain that control is essential and that the quickest round will not be achieved by the rider whose pony gallops fastest, but by the rider who rides the neatest track while maintaining rhythm and balance at as fast a speed as possible.

With impetuous competition ponies it may be unwise to practise this: as unless the fences are high and impressive, any increase in speed may result in careless jumping. Suggest that their riders practise riding a careful neat track. This will leave the ponies settled in their minds for future competitions.

With most rides the shortened course may be jumped against the clock, the Coach/Instructor timing each round. Riders who achieve good results can finish, and begin to warm down their ponies. Those who do not manage to ride neatly and accurately should immediately try another round, after discussing their problems with the Coach/Instructor. In almost every case this extra round will be better and faster. Even sluggish ponies who do not like jumping become more enthusiastic, while their riders feel a distinct sense of achievement. This is a good note on which to end a lesson. The ride should walk on a long rein around the fences to warm down their ponies.

NOTE:

The less controllable show-jumping ponies often have exceptional natural jumping ability which has been over-exploited, their early training having been neglected. Their riders are brave, but have little control. Therefore if such a pony begins to settle and 'listen' to his rider, the rider must improve himself and give the correct aids, or the pony will misunderstand and may start to refuse. Beware of making radical changes to successful partnerships during the competition season.

The thinking rider will quickly realise the long-term importance of improving his riding.

(c) Riding Across Country

General Considerations

Mention of going across country conjures up visions of galloping over fields with successive lines of beautiful, straightforward fences, and hounds in front. Teaching cross-country riding is a very different matter. The rider must be taught:

(a) To ride at a specific speed in cold blood away from and towards the rest of the ride.

(b) To jump straightforward fences at a basic cross-country speed and tricky fences from slow speeds.
(c) To ride on an accurate line towards, over, and away from a fence. (To practise this, *see* Exercise 8 on page 70.)
(d) To jump related fences on the flat and on different ground levels. (*See* 'Doubles', page 68.)
(e) To jump on gradients (*see* page 69) and over drop fences.
(f) To jump ditches and water.
(g) To ride through water.

Correct riding with a secure position is essential across country. This security and balance is achieved by the rider moving their seat back and just above the saddle, a secure lower leg, the heel just below the toe, and the rider's shoulders not in front of their knees. A secure balanced position between fences takes time to achieve, but the feeling of security, with improved rhythm and control, will increase the confidence and competence of both rider and pony.

Speed Control

The ride should learn to jump a straightforward, solid-looking fence at each individual pony's optimum cross-country pace. To practise this, the ride should line up well on the landing side of the fence. Each rider should make a long approach and should continue on the landing side in the same rhythmical cross-country pace. Next the ride should practise jumping a low fence from a trot with a short approach, then turning either way immediately after the fence.

The Course

At competitions, the course must be walked by riders on foot, but at rallies, if a course is available it can be 'walked' by the ride on their ponies. All fences can then be discussed and practised over as you go along. It sometimes helps to give timid ponies a lead. Remember that because of differences in type and ability, the ponies may tackle some fences in different ways, choosing whichever way is easiest for them.

At each fence discuss:
(a) The line of approach.
(b) The speed of approach and how far away that speed should be established.
(c) The take-off and landing zones.
(d) The line of the recovery stride.
(e) The impulsion needed in the recovery stride. (This is especially important in an uphill combination.)
(f) The line and speed to be taken towards the next fence.

(g) The importance of maintaining contact and of moving confidently forward in the final stage before take-off: even if the fence is a 2 m. drop approached in walk!

(h) How to tackle multiple fences. Look at the positions of the flags and the different ways in which the fences may be jumped. Consider this with each individual rider, as the fences may pose different problems for each of them, and different lines of approach, jump and recovery may be chosen.

Fences with Obscure Landings

These include obstacles which entail jumping from light to dark, into shadows or woods, and 'into space'. They often cause ponies to refuse.

Before expecting a pony to take off it is necessary to allow him to see what is on the landing side. This is achieved by making a slow approach but with strong rhythm and impulsion, either in trot or slow canter. In this way he has time to see where he is going and still has the impetus to go there.

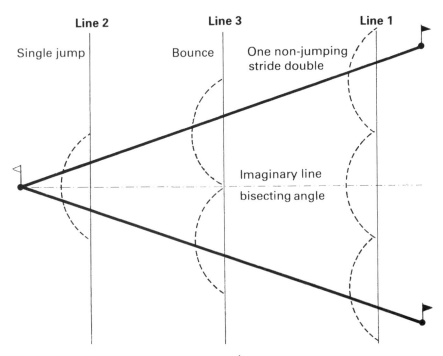

Fig. 28 Three different ways to jump a corner fence.

Ditches

These often cause problems, especially if rider and pony look down into the bottom of the ditch. If the ditch is in front of the fence, rider and pony should concentrate firmly on the fence. If it is just a plain ditch they should concentrate on the *landing side*. If the pony shies and decreases the speed, his rider must be quick to maintain impulsion. If his hocks are engaged he can still jump the ditch however slowly he is going. *See* also 'Ditches', page 70.

Jumping into Water

Only practise this if the water is shallow, has a sound bottom, and is far too wide (over 8 m.) for the ponies to jump. Walk the ride through the water and allow the ponies to stand and splash a little until they are completely familiar with it. Then progress slowly, from walking and then trotting off the bank into the water, to jumping a small fence.

In competitions water should be approached in the same way as for 'Fences with Obscure Landings' (described above) except that if the fence is small the speed may be slower. If there is a steep approach or a large drop into the water, it might be safer to walk.

Corner Fences (Fig. 28)

When built on flat terrain, it is possible to negotiate these in three different ways:

LINE 1   One non-jumping stride between the elements. This line should always be chosen unless the rider is capable of riding on a completely accurate line through the obstacle.

LINE 2   Both elements cleared in one jump. The approach should be on a line to an imaginary fence which bisects the angle made by the two elements. It is unwise to choose this approach if the pony is likely to run out or to veer sideways as he jumps. Accuracy is essential.

LINE 3   'Bouncing' over the obstacle. Plan the line according to the 'bounce' distance which each pony takes when schooling over bounce fences of this height. If such schooling has not been carried out, this plan is not advisable.

Corner fences can be in many different forms. The lines shown in Fig. 28 are not always straight, and the angle of the corners will vary from being very narrow and inviting, to being too wide to jump. Check the position of the flags, consider all the possibilities, and judge each case on its own merits.

Tantivies

These are useful for encouraging the confidence of both rider and pony. If an assistant has a suitable horse he may act as 'field-master', leading the ride round the cross-country course. Otherwise the ride may be sent round in groups, pairs or singly according to how they will manage best. The Coach/Instructor should be careful to maintain control and to keep the ride in sight at all times. He or she should never take the risk of allowing riders to jump too fast into quarries, combinations, or other tricky fences—which could cause horrific falls. Riders whose ponies are inclined to run away should be sent singly; and the faint-hearted—whether rider or pony—should be sent with a combination who will provide a satisfactory lead.

Determination

The tantivy can be used as fun to finish off a junior lesson, but for the more advanced it should only be used as a means to an end, as they should learn to make their ponies go in cold blood—i.e. without the encouragement of company. This takes far more skill and determination, and teaches the important lesson that no sensible pony goes across country alone without clear, concise, and emphatic guidance from the rider.

Conditioning and Fitness

It should be made clear that ponies need to be considerably fitter for cross-country events than for normal hacking. During the cross-country lesson, time should be taken to discuss suitable training programmes, thereby ensuring that the ponies are adequately prepared for any strenuous events for which they are entered.

Cooling Off/Warming Down

As always, the lesson should end on a happy note, perhaps with the ride having satisfactorily jumped one or two straightforward fences. As the ponies will have been galloping, they should be dismounted and led with girths loosened and stirrups up, until they are dry and settled. The Coach/Instructor should ensure that the riders understand how to look after their ponies both before and after they have been galloping. It is important to discuss the special care needed in feeding and watering during training and on the day of the competition.

For the More Experienced Coach/ Instructor

18 School Movements Performed in Various Ways: Formation Riding

School movements performed in various ways under a competent Coach/Instructor are interesting and fun for the ride. They may also be used in a suitable order to produce a formation ride. First make sure that you can organise the ride, as described in Chapter 4 (page 26).

Secondly, practise new movements with matches on a tray before trying them out at the rally. Use one match per rider.

Most movements may be performed by the ride in the following ways:
'In single file'.
'In succession'.
'By rides'.
'Double ride'.
'Whole ride'.
'In succession' and *'whole ride'* are explained in Chapter 4 (pages 28–9).

Before being able to carry out more complicated movements with your ride you must know, and the ride must understand, the following:

Numbering
This means that each member of the ride calls out his number. The words of command are: *'Ride from the front, over your inside shoulder—number'*. The leading file turns his head to the inside and says *'One'*, whereupon the rider behind him turns his head and says *'Two'*, the next *'Three'*, and so on, until the rear of the ride is reached. It is sometimes advisable to repeat this.

Proving
This means that each rider 'proves' that he has memorised his number. When his number is called he responds by transferring his reins and whip to his outside hand, then raises his inside arm, straight, forward, and level with his shoulder.

Dividing into Rides
This, which is for work by rides, means dividing the class, after numbering, into equal groups. Words of command might be 'Numbers 1 to 4 are Number 1 ride, Numbers 5 to 8 are Number 2 ride'. Alternatively, the riders may be numbered from the front in fours (or twos, threes or fives).

Double Ride

This means that the ride is divided into two from the front, odd numbers in one ride and even numbers in the other. Odd numbers are responsible for the pace, and even numbers for the dressing. Each ride follows its own leading file.

Dressing

This means keeping in line or in position during a movement. *'Dressing by the left'* means that every rider glances to his left and keeps in line with the rider at the left end of the row. Each rider is responsible for keeping his own dressing. Unless commanded otherwise, dressing is always carried out by keeping in line with the riders on the side towards which the turn is made.

Arena or School

It is usual to use the word 'school' when giving commands (e.g. *'Turning across the school'*). 'School' is therefore used in this chapter when discussing the control of the ride, although it is recognised that the riding area would generally be an outdoor arena.

NOTE: When working in the school in opposite directions, riders should pass left hand to left hand.

Working by Rides

• Number the whole ride from the front and divide it into smaller rides: e.g. a ride of 9 into 3 rides of 3; a ride of 8 into 2 rides of 4.
• Check that everyone knows to which ride they belong.
• When performing a movement by rides each member of the named ride obeys the executive command at the same moment and keeps his dressing from the rider on the side to which they have turned: i.e. if the ride is turned to the right, dressing is kept from the rider on the right.
• When manoeuvring by rides with the riders coming towards you, watch where the leading rider of the first ride moves off the track. Then time your executive commands to subsequent rides so that their leaders leave the track at the same place.
• If the rides are going away from you, check that the rear file of each ride turns in the same place.
• If you turn the second and subsequent rides too early, the riders will be baulked when they reach the track. If you turn them too late, gaps will appear between the rides.

Now try:

Turning by Rides (Fig. 29)

Turns across the school should be ordered as the rides approach the end of the long side. The riders in each ride turn on command, simultaneously, staying on the same rein and having plenty of the next long side to ride down after they have turned. Note that Number 4 in each ride becomes the leading file. To bring back Number 1 to the front, turn by rides again.

COMMAND: *'By rides, turning across the school, Number 1 ride turn... Number 2 ride turn, etc.'*

Double Ride Work

When turning the rides down the centre line in pairs, even numbers must dress alongside their odd numbers: i.e. 1 and 2 together (Fig. 30).

A Drill Ride

The following drill ride is fun for everyone. Leading-rein rides can perform it at the walk. Turn the ride down the centre line in pairs. (*See* Fig. 30).

To bring the ride down the centre in fours:
COMMAND: *'First pair to the left, second pair to the right.'*
RESULT: As the pairs reach the opposite end of the arena they turn alternatively left and right.
COMMAND: *'By fours down the centre.'*
RESULT: As each pair reaches the centre marker they turn, as fours, down the centre.

This may continue until eights or sixteens come in a line down the centre, at which point the Coach/Instructor might command a halt and salute.

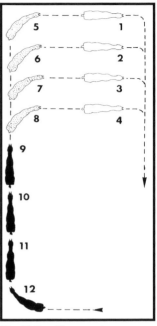

Fig. 29 By rides, turning across the school.

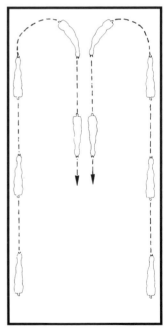

Fig. 30 Double ride turning down the centre in pairs

To revert to a single line from fours:

As the fours proceed down the centre line:

COMMAND: *'Pairs to the left and right.'*

RESULT: At the end of the arena the two on the left turn left, the two on the right turn right.

As the pairs are halfway up the side:

COMMAND: *'By pairs down the centre.'*

RESULT: The left pair will turn first, with the right pair turning in behind them; then the next left pair, and so on.

As the pairs proceed down the centre:

COMMAND: *'Odd numbers turn left, even numbers turn right.'*

RESULT: The ride follows the command.

COMMAND: *'In single file down the centre, form a single ride.'*

RESULT: The ride turns into its original order. Make sure that Number 1 rider knows that he must turn in front of Number 2 rider on to the centre line.

COMMAND: *'Leading file on the left (or right) rein.'*

RESULT: The ride follows the leading file on to the outer track.

NOTE: Before carrying out the above in trot or canter, consider the size of the arena, the size of the ponies, and the difficulty of the turns.

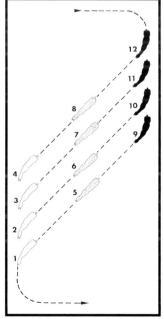

Fig. 31 By rides, inclining across the school

Inclining Across the School

COMMAND: *'By rides, inclining across the school, Number 1 ride—inwards incline.'*

RESULT: On the word 'incline', each member of Number 1 ride moves simultaneously off the track. The dressing should be taken from the leading file. The shoulders of all riders should be in line (Fig. 31).

Four Ways of Performing Small Circles
(1) In Single File

COMMAND: *'In single file, circle on to the centre line and return to the track, leading file circle.'*

RESULT: In single file the ride describes a semi-circle on to the centre line (between A and C) and proceeds (towards A or C) until the given command *'Away'*, when remaining in single file, the ride describes another semi-circle back onto the track and goes large on the original rein.

(2) By Rides

COMMAND: *'By rides, circle on to the centre line and return to the track. Number 1 ride commence'*... *'Number 2 ride commence'*... etc.

RESULT: On command, each ride describes a semi-circle to the centre line and proceeds in single file on the centre line until commanded *'Away'*. Then each ride describes another semi-circle back on to the track and goes large on the original rein. (Fig 32).

As explained fully on page 101, every ride must circle at the same place.

(3) By the Whole Ride

COMMAND: *'Whole ride, circle on to the centre line and return to the track, ride circle.'*
RESULT: Every rider simultaneously describes a semi-circle on to the centre line and proceeds in single file until commanded *'Away'*. Then each rider describes another semi-circle back onto the track and goes large on the original rein.

(4) Double Ride

The ride will have been divided into a double ride. The leading files will be nearing the end of the long sides when the executive command is given.

COMMAND: *'Double ride, circle on to the centre line and return to the track. Rides circle'*.
RESULT: The rides circle in towards each other, slotting in to the gaps (the double distance) when they reach the centre line (Fig. 33). The rides proceed in single file on the centre line until the command *'Away'*. They then turn in alternate directions, describing semi-circles and returning to their respective long sides, going large in their original directions.

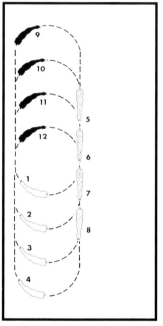

Fig. 32 By rides, circling on to the centre line.

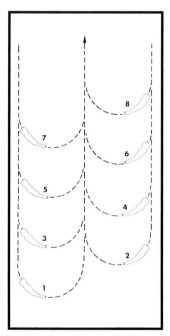

Fig. 33 Double ride circling on to the centre line.

Points to Remember
- Explain any new exercises carefully. Demonstrate them if necessary, then ask if the ride understands.
- New exercises should be ridden and established at the walk before attempting them at the trot (or perhaps, later, at canter).
- It is better for the ride to perform single exercises well than to be confused with work which is too complicated.
- Each rider should ride forward with thought and care, to keep his place in the ride, and to help the other riders to keep their places.
- Encourage members to work on their ponies individually.
- Formation riding can be hard work for the average pony and should not be continued for too long.
- Double ride work is an enjoyable way of finishing off a lesson.
- Practised, and set to music, a series of movements can make an impressive display or formation ride.
- If things go wrong, don't panic. Halt the ride, reorganise, and try again at the walk.

Tricycling
Tricycling provides a large class with the security of single file conditions and the advantages of individual practice. The ride can carry out quite complicated movements without any command from the Coach/Instructor. Although most valuable when taking a large group of members, it can be interesting and fun for all rides.

1. The command 'Commence tricycling' is given as the leader approaches the short side of the arena.
2. In the corner, the leader turns in the normal way, remaining on the outer track, but the second and third riders do not follow. They turn with the leader at the same time, and cross the short side of the arena shoulder to shoulder.
3. The next right or left turn brings them once more into single file in reverse order.

Fig. 34 shows three positions of the white horse, the grey, and the black while tricycling around the arena.

The changing from single file on the long side to three abreast on the short side is automatic, and is repeated by the riders until they are told to stop tricycling.

Once the ride has grasped the basic principle and has negotiated the first turn across the side of the school, the groups of three, and each rider's position in his group, will have been established without the need to number the ride off 'by threes'.

All groups of three follow exactly in the tracks of the first three; i.e. in the first corner, Number 4 rides into the corner and turns, remaining on the outer track, while Number 5 and 6 turn alongside him. This is repeated throughout the ride.

Having established his position in the group of three, each rider will notice that he follows the line of the rider in the same relative position of the group in front, i.e. Numbers 2, 5 and 8 will follow on in the same tracks (with plenty of room between them).

Once the ride has mastered tricycling around the school (riding down the long side in single file and across the short side three abreast) other movements can be introduced. The ride might perform inclining (Fig. 35), large circles (Fig. 36), half figures-of-eight (Fig. 37), serpentines, loops, and many others. The leading three choose among themselves the direction or movement. The Coach/Instructor's commands should be kept to a minimum. Tricycling may be performed to music.

Points to Remember

• Every rider must concentrate, must think ahead, and must follow exactly in the track of his corresponding number.

• His corresponding number is never the one just in front; he must follow the third horse in front.

• In turning across the arena the dressing is taken from the inside rider.

• The inside rider must adjust his pace so that having turned across the arena he fits in again at the correct distance behind the group in front. (He is now the leader of his own group).

• Riders in each group must always be the same distance from the long sides of the arena as their group leader; they turn away together, and must therefore arrive together at the side. This is particularly important when moving across the school as in the change of rein.

The advantage of tricycling is that it enables the Coach/Instructor to concentrate on the riding, but he or she should avoid making too many comments during the exercise.

The same system may be used for *bicycling*, when two riders, instead of three, perform, as in tricycling.

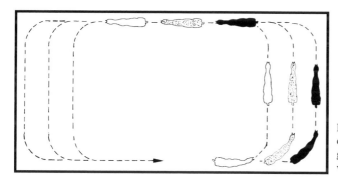

Fig. 34 Three positions of the white horse, the grey, and the black while tricycling.

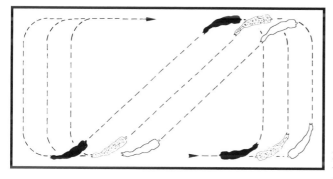

Fig. 35 Inclining while tricycling.

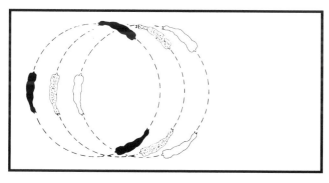

Fig. 36 Circling while tricycling.

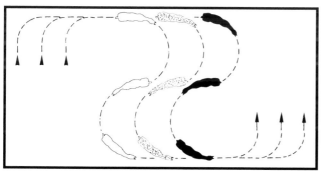

Fig. 37 Half figures-of-eight while tricycling.

Producing a Formation Ride

Most of the movements described in this chapter are suitable for inclusion in a formation ride. Consider:

• The numbers of riders.
• The size of the ponies.
• The colours of the ponies.
• The size of the arena.
• Where the spectators will be.
• Where the salute should be made.
• The time allowed.

Using movements suitable for the standard of the ride, write down the correct commands for your formation ride. Prepare suitable music and equipment. The volume and tone should be reasonable. Scottish reels, Irish jigs, and Country and Western music are generally suitable.

Consider what everyone will wear. Matching sweaters are effective.

If possible, use a member of your ride to try the movements and to check how long the display will take.

With the Ride

1. Arrange the riders in an appropriate order.
2. Practise the ride at the walk, teaching a few movements at a time.
3. Go through the whole series at the walk.
4. Practise at the appropriate paces.
5. Try it with the music.

Simple exercises performed well and accurately look better than complicated ones performed badly.

To ensure a successful performance the Coach/Instructor must ALWAYS COMMAND THE RIDE.

19 The Difference Between a Coach and an Instructor

The technical knowledge of a coach or an instructor should be the same. Both will be comfortable and familiar with the information that they are passing on. The difference lies in the way that the knowledge is conveyed to the rider.

Good instructors have always been good coaches, but it is not a skill that comes easily to everyone like so, like many skills, it will require thought, preparation and practise.

At the extreme end of the spectrum is a military figure, shouting all commands to a repressed ride, or a coach who whispers to the team in the corner of the locker room. The modern version of the coach will be listening to the riders, and encouraging them to take ownership of what they want to learn.

The old adage 'Be told something and forget, do something and remember', applies well to coaching, although the 'do something' might be asking questions, discussing, and recalling, as well as riding.

When checking the tack at the beginning of any ride you can discover what your rider would like to do with the pony/horse, both today and in the future. This will give you that rider's short- and long-term goals.

As this is a group lesson the subject of rhythm may already have been chosen but your rider wants to know how to get past the pigs at the end of the lane. Helping your rider to know when to notice the rhythm changes on approaching the pigs may help your rider achieve their goal of passing the pigs without the horse/pony spinning around. Almost all lessons can aid riders towards their individual goals if time is taken to show the riders where this lesson can help them. An inexperienced rider would be unlikely to make the link between rhythm in an arena and a horse/pony slowing up on approaching the end of the lane.

Assessing the Ride

All good instructors assess the ride at the start of the lesson; this was the warm-up period. Coach/Instructors will also use this time to ask questions of their riders, to check their understanding of previous work, and to assess how much they are feeling of what their pony/horse is doing. If the coach asks, 'Tell me what you thought about that transition', it will help the coach know at what level to begin teaching that rider.

These types of question throughout the session will help the riders to think about what the horse/pony is doing. Once they are aware of the problems the next question is, 'What are you going to do about it?' Their answers will be quickly discussed and praised and/or help given. By the end of the session each rider will be able to make an assessment of a transition and will have themselves, with help, have decided upon an improvement.

As, throughout, the riders have been involved and shared in the decisions, they have begun to take ownership of their learning; by doing this they are less likely to 'be told and forget'.

Explanation and Demonstration

Following the initial introduction and warm up/assessment will come the explanation of the new subject. A coach will make great efforts to 'sell' the new subject to the riders. Early explanations from each rider on their goals, both for today and long term, will be of assistance to the coach on how to '*sell*' the subject to each rider. A supple horse is so much nicer to ride but, for the inexperienced, who have never had the opportunity to ride a trained horse, the effort to achieve this may not seem worthwhile. However, selling the idea to the rider as a way of achieving better time against the clock, may make it seem worthwhile to try to see if the next jump-off round is faster. Everyone works better when the outcome may have advantage for them rather than seeming to be just an obscure idea that the instructor has suggested.

Practice

The main body of the lesson is to practise the new subject. Question to ensure understanding has taken place before you begin. Discuss and comment constructively throughout the lesson. Consistently start from the point of asking, '*What was good about...*' Follow this up by asking how it could be improved, or by advising a route to try. Inexperienced riders will need to be taught at times, as they do not have the skill to isolate the problem and solution, but, if you have taught the point clearly, next time they should be able to tell you what has happened. It may be more familiar to shout instructions, but the object of a lesson is to empower the riders so they know what is wrong and how to correct it.

Throughout the lesson position corrections should be continual. However, rather than the well-known shout of, '*Keep your legs back,*' try replacing it with, '*At what points around the arena are you thinking of your leg position?*' The responsibility of improvement is firmly placed back with the rider, with consistent constructive comment and praise for the effort shown.

During the lesson, stand behind as well as to the side of the riders, and chose only one area per rider to concentrate on at a time. It is not productive for a rider to try to improve the rhythm, bend, leg and hand position all at the same time. Embed one improvement before looking for another.

Feedback

At the end of a lesson there should be time taken for feedback. The riders may have questions to ask the coach, and the coach will ask enough questions to find out whether the riders have (a) really understood the lesson, and (b) how that lesson will help the individual towards their short- and long-term goals. They should also be asked how they will practise the new skill at home.

Self-Evaluation

Coaches will think about each lesson that they have taught. Did the riders have fun and enjoy their lesson? Begin with what went well, and why. Could you store what you did to replicate it again in another place? Then consider what might have gone better. Every lesson can be enhanced, so search for what to improve and what might be changed for an even better outcome next time.

Finally, consider the instructor approach, of telling the riders what the instructor thinks they should learn and how they should work. This has produced many fine riders, but it may have lost some who were not so dedicated or professional. The good instructor/coach has always involved the riders in their own improvement and listened to the rider's opinions. More thought given to '*how*' the information is conveyed, will develop the coaching skill within all instructors, and promote better understanding by the riders.

20 Improving Communication

A message conveyed clearly is far more likely to be understood and acted upon than muddled information, so it is to both the Coach/Instructors' and riders' benefit, that the Coach/Instructor is easily understood. This is not only the ability to make oneself heard at the far end of the arena.

The way the Coach/Instructor is dressed is one sort of communication. Clothes fit for purpose, clean and tidy, reflect respect for the Pony Club as an organisation and the riders in their lesson. Dirty clothes suggest that this occasion, and these riders, were not worth the bother of changing.

Listening to riders is vital. Showing a desire to listen, and understand what they are telling you, will convey an interest in them as people, not just as unimportant beings who happen to move ponies around. A true interest in each rider will enhance that rider's self esteem and confidence—strangely a more important goal than a straight line down the centre.

Look at the rider as you speak to them; eye contact is important. The riders will know that you are listening to what they say, and they will be able to watch your facial expression and judge whether you are attending to what they say, or merely planning your next move.

Enthusiasm is infectious, and is a quality held by all good Coach/ Instructors. Lack of enthusiasm makes for a boring session, and lowers both the spirits and self esteem of the riders.

Most people will have spent time with an enthusiastic person, who seems to have a genuine interest in you, and discusses with you how to improve. Compare this with the bored teacher, who obviously has no interest in you, and presents a subject that you cannot see as relevant to you. The question to ask is, *'Which one would you like to learn from?'* To ensure that you are the obvious answer, consider how you communicate from the riders' point of view.

21 A Riding Lesson or Traffic Direction?

When a rider sits correctly the aids can be applied effectively, and the horse's way of going will improve. This is one of the great truths of riding. The question that follows is how to achieve riders sitting well? The answer is perseverance on the part of the Coach/Instructor and effort by the rider.

It is difficult to sit correctly, and initially the riders will not know when, or not, they are sitting in the correct position. So it is up to the Coach/Instructor to persevere in helping the rider to feel what is right or wrong, so they can make the corrections not only under the Coach/ Instructor's eye, but also alone, following the lesson.

Many inexperienced Coach/Instructors find it difficult to move the riders around the school and teach positional corrections at the same time. A usable plan is to give each rider a correction to work on. Then make a traffic direction, such as *'change the rein'*.

Having changed the rein the Coach/Instructor will ask each rider what they are practising in their position, which allows them to know that each rider understands his individual goal. Then there may be a command for a loop to be ridden and whilst this happens each rider will receive comment on their position.

The lesson will progress in this way: correction, traffic control manoeuvre, correction and question on position, traffic control, correction, etc. This work is like a sandwich, so on each side of the movements there is assistance in improving the rider's position. This degree of input is vital in order to make rapid improvement. One or two comments to a rider within the lesson will soon be forgotten; it is the sheer persistence of the Coach/Instructor which will embed the knowledge of the mistake, why it is advantageous to try to abolish the problem and what it feels like to be sitting correctly.

When assessing the rider's position look at them from more than one angle. Follow the faults in the extremities back into the core of the body. Is the rider looking down and tipped forward? To tell this rider to look up is not helping the root of the problem. If this rider is told to sit on his seat and take the shoulders above the hips almost certainly the head will come up. Many faults in the legs and arms derive from the position of the seat in the saddle.

Having decided the origin of the fault, discuss this with your rider, even at D Test they are ready for a simple version. Then work on one point at a time, so riders are able to concentrate on that point until they have remembered the feel of the new improvement. Recognising the feel of this improvement is important if they are going to be able to work on their position after the session.

Most Coach/Instructors feel they have offered lots of seat correction, but experience shows that if an assistant watches, and counts the number of seat corrections to each individual, frequently it is not more than two or three within each lesson, completely insufficient for an hour's session.

Lungeing is an excellent way of improving riders' positions, but as it is generally a one to one activity is not practical in a rally situation. So the onus is on the Coach/Instructor; it is only your input that will improve the positions of a new generation of riders.

22 Four Rides Within a Ride

At any Pony Club function you are lucky if you are given a ride of matching standards. The DC or Organiser will have tried their best, but what was a cohesive group in the Easter holidays now consists of one rider who has been bought a smart competition pony and had many lessons and is above the standard of the others. There is a little middle group that go well together, but there is also one of their friends who has been bought a young horse, of which she is rather nervous, and which is too big for her. The last is a brand new member, who has almost no theory of riding to speak of, but is brave and under-mounted.

Ideally these riders would be in four different groups, but it is your task to work them together. In these circumstances, which could be the majority of Pony Club rallies, your chosen subject for the lesson is like wrapping paper, going around and giving a common theme, from which your riders will have individual goals.

Supposing turns and circles are the subjects of your lesson. The explanation could be broken down by asking the middle group the aids for a turn. Repeat these in a clarified form to allow the new member to hear them for the first time, then ask your more educated rider whether she would refine the basic aid in any way.

Before moving off ask each member of the ride what their aim is when practising the turns. This should be different for many of the riders. The more advanced pony may be working on maintaining impulsion and straightness through the turns. The main block of riders may be working on their pony's suppleness and bend, the young horse will be working on rhythm and the new member will be practising applying the aids in correct sequence.

The riders should work in open order; little is to be gained from trailing one behind another. Riding individually can be carefully introduced from early on, and allows and encourages all riders to work their own ponies and horses.

This approach allows the Coach/Instructor to offer constructive advice to the riders as individuals, asking them to comment on their pony's way of going at the different levels.

By working in this way the riders have been challenged at their own level, and have progressed from the point where they started. Otherwise only the young horse rider and the new member would have had a meaningful session, as all the others could make turns before they even arrived in your arena.

23 The Scale of Training

Photographs of Pony Club ponies fifty years ago show that they worked longer and lower and had less top line than their counterparts today. The courses jumped now are more technical, asking for a greater degree of suppleness. Despite these changes, few Pony Club riders, and only some Coach/Instructors, have an overarching plan which will lead towards these necessary changes.

When building a house that is expected to stand for many years the builders use a plan. This plan will start with the foundations and progress upwards to the roofline. A modern house with no foundations would not be expected to last, and without a plan the outcome would probably be haphazard.

Many riders begin to school their ponies and horses without a plan of progression, and without any foundations in place. The result is almost certainly haphazard and unreliable.

Germany has for many years followed a plan, called 'The Scale of Training', which has produced Olympic Champions and hundreds of other well-trained horses, that are a pleasure to ride and reliable under the stress of competition.

Each part of the scale acts as foundation or prerequisite for the next, so when the first, rhythm, is in place the horse is ready to begin working on the next. When introducing any new work to your pony/horse, such as leg yielding, you will start again to work on the rhythm, whilst when working in normal canter the aim might be contact.

Rhythm	The regularity of the beat within the gait. Until a horse or pony can trot or canter in a regular rhythm it is almostrove any other part of his way of going.
Suppleness	Both from side to side, left and right, and longitudinally so the pony can begin to work in a rounded shape, and does not try to resist when the rider gives an aid. To achieve suppleness the pony must be relaxed and free from tension.
Contact	Does the weight of reins feel the same into both hands? Does it feel elastic? Is there more weight into one hand or the other, or is the horse bearing down on your hands? The hind legs should be connected by a band of muscles along the back, neck and poll allowing the rider to feel the forward energy equally into both hands.
Impulsion	The energy the horse or pony steps forwards with, whilst maintaining his balance. The first training aim just has rhythm; this aim has rhythm and balance and energy, because the hind legs are further under the body enabling the horse to spring forwards easily.
Straightness	As the horse or pony becomes more supple, balanced and energetic he will find it easier to work straight, so within every movement the hind legs will follow in the tracks that the front legs have created
Collection	Once the pony or horse has all the previous training aims in place he is able to balance himself better and better, and can now take more of his, and your, weight over his hind legs, and perform with greater power.

These training aims also apply to jumping; it is very handy to have a horse who can collect when approaching a big fence off a tight corner!

The Scale is introduced gradually to horses, and since the revised Pony Club Tests in 2010 the Scale is introduced to the riders in the same way, starting with rhythm at D+. This should lead to riders understanding a route along which to train their ponies and horses, and it is as relevant to a happy hacker as it is to a keenly competitive rider.

24 Smart Targets

It is easier to structure a work programme for riders if a smart target is applied. 'SMART' is an acronym for Specific, Measurable, Achievable, Relevant and Time-scaled. Probably all Coach/Instructors start camp week with the intention of improving the ride's jumping; this is worthwhile, but will not be as focused as if they have a precise goal, or smart target. Supposing the ride was hoping to take their B Test in August, the smart target would work like this:

Specific   The riders will need to jump a show jumping round of 90 cm. for the B Test.

Measurable The fences will include a double and be 90 cm. high.

Achievable This height is within the capacity of all the ride.

Relevant   All six wish to take their B Test.

Time-scaled Five days in camp.

The advantage of the smart target is to focus the sessions; no longer is the idea just to improve the jumping. The ride has a target, specifically to ride a round of show jumps, at a certain height and including a double. They can all jump 90 cm. so it will be achievable, and all will be happy to work on this as it is relevant for their B Test, and as they are at camp for five days that is the timescale.

Great satisfaction can be gained from achieving the smart target, or a short-term goal. As ever with rides, not every rider might be taking their B Test this year, but if half the ride wanted to jump a course of 80 cm. on their young horse/old pony the smart target could remain virtually the same, with the Coach/Instructor just reducing the size of the fences after half the ride had jumped.

25 Trotting-Poles and Gymnastic Jumping Exercises

Trotting-poles and gymnastic exercises are useful training aids in teaching the horse and rider to jump. They are most valuable during private lessons, Pony Club camps or regular lessons with horses and riders who are known to you. It should be said however, that since gymnastic exercises require fences set at closely related distances, the problems of using them at working rallies sometimes outweigh the advantages.

They are not suitable for the child's first pony who, with his novice rider, will hardly manage enough impulsion to negotiate a line of related fences correctly. The average Pony Club ride consists of ponies of different types with varying strides, so valuable time will be lost adjusting the distances. However, as long as the ride is well enough advanced to control the speed and tempo of the trot, useful lessons with trotting-poles may be given. Should conditions be right, and should enough time and be available, gymnastic jumping exercises might then be performed. An enclosed area is preferable for jumping, and is essential for work without holding the reins.

Trotting-Poles

Trotting over a series of poles on the ground is an extension of correct work on the flat and is useful because:

For the pony:
- It improves the trot by increasing the activity of the shoulders and hindquarters.
- It regulates the length and rhythm of the stride, thus improving the balance.
- As the pony looks down to see and avoid the poles he is encouraged to stretch and round his back.

For the rider:
- It teaches the feel and tempo of a steady, rhythmical active trot.
- It improves his position and balance as he learns to stay in harmony with his pony.
- It teaches a correct approach, not interfering with the pony except to maintain a rhythmical trot on the correct line of approach.
- It teaches the feel of a light contact with the pony's mouth, which should be maintained at all times, especially when the pony takes the bit and stretches his head out and down. The rider should allow the pony to take this extra rein without moving his weight in the saddle.

Riders who have difficulty in maintaining their positions should use neckstraps, or they will upset the balance and rhythm of their ponies. The neckstrap should be fitted so that it is conveniently placed for the rider to hold without having to move his weight.

Work over trotting-poles is generally carried out at rising trot, and should be performed on either diagonal. More advanced riders may use sitting trot.

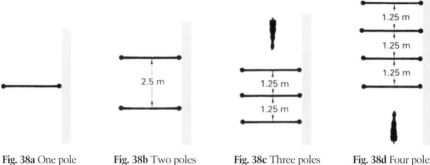

Fig. 38a One pole   **Fig. 38b** Two poles   **Fig. 38c** Three poles   **Fig. 38d** Four poles

Equipment

A minimum of four poles will be needed; but with five trotting-poles, two pairs of stands, and seven additional poles, a suitable combination of trotting-poles and fences may be built if required.

Positioning the Equipment

Position the trotting-poles alongside a hedge or fence or the wall of an indoor school. This will help to keep the ponies straight.

Method

The ride should first walk and then take rising trot over a single pole with the Coach/Instructor watching to see that each pony negotiates the pole calmly and without breaking the rhythm (Fig. 38a).

The ride may then trot over the poles with two trotting strides between them (2.5 m. or approx. 8 ft. for ponies). (Fig. 38b).

Never trot the ride over two poles at a trotting stride (1.25 m. or approx. 4 ft. apart) as the ponies might try to jump the two poles.

Next, add a third pole midway between the first two, thus giving three poles at trotting distance. (Fig. 38c).

The Coach/Instructor must watch carefully to see that the distances between the poles are correct for the ponies, as although he or she may start with a measured 1.25 m. distance between each pole the distances will probably need adjusting, so that they are correct enough for the ride to trot over easily. Poles which are knocked out of place must be put back.

Having established that the distance between the poles is comfortable for the ponies in the ride, add a fourth pole, about 1.25 m. after the third (Fig. 38d). Further poles added at correct distances help to develop rhythm and balance.

Change the rein frequently. At this stage the poles may be approached in either direction.

If you have time, remove one of the inside poles to see whether the ponies maintain their rhythm and stride when there is a pole missing.

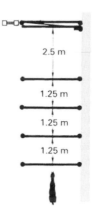

Then replace it.

Each rider should try to maintain the rhythm of the trot through the poles and on round the arena.

Trotting-Poles with One Jump

If the ride is negotiating the trotting-poles satisfactorily and if the same distances between the poles are correct for all the ponies in the ride, a small jump may be built about 2.5 m. (8 ft.) from the last of the four trotting-poles (Fig. 39).

Use a substantial pole, with crossed poles or a diagonal pole underneath it, and a take-off pole on the ground a few inches in front. Measure from the last of the trotting-poles to the take-off pole.

Fig. 39 Four trotting-poles and one jump.

Each pony in turn should trot over the poles and jump the fence at the end.

Check that they take off from both hind legs in unison; a sign that the hocks are correctly engaged. The riders should sit quietly and in harmony with the movement of the ponies.

Sometimes quite startling improvement can be made by taking the riders' minds off the actual jump. Getting them to sing, or to concentrate on some object ahead, can reduce the tension transmitted from them to their ponies, and the wildest pony will often settle and perform calmly.

Trotting-Poles with Two or Three Jumps

If the above-mentioned exercise is performed satisfactorily a second fence may be built (for ponies, about 5 m. or 16 ft.) away from the first fence. Fig. 40). Imperial measurements and horse distances are in the Appendix.

The ponies should trot over the poles, jump the first fence, take one canter stride, and jump the second fence. If they manage this calmly and fluently, and if the area is big enough, a third, slightly higher, fence may be added about 5.5 m. (18 ft.) from the second (Fig.41, overleaf).

The distance between the second and third fence should be slightly longer than the distance between the first and second fence, as by then the ponies will have established a stronger canter rhythm. The distances between the fences are approximate. Use your judgement to adjust them until they are correct for the ponies.

This permutation, with two, three or more fences, may be used as a base for many valuable exercises. Once the ponies have trotted over the poles—provided the tempo and rhythm are maintained and the distances are correct—there is little to go wrong. Thus ponies and riders learn to relax during the approach and over the fences; and the riders develop feel and appreciation for the movement and power of their ponies.

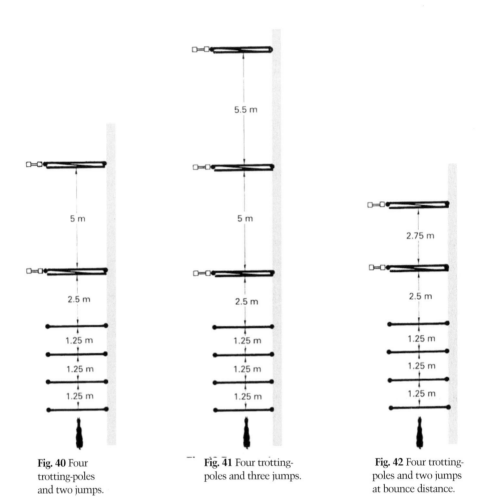

Fig. 40 Four trotting-poles and two jumps.

Fig. 41 Four trotting-poles and three jumps.

Fig. 42 Four trotting-poles and two jumps at bounce distance.

Physical Exercises for Riders While Jumping

Once the ponies are performing fluently over the previous line of poles and fences, the riders may perform exercises to improve their positions, such as: each rider ties his reins in a knot. He then trots over the poles, and as the pony jumps the first fence the rider loses the reins and either puts his hands on his hips, strokes the pony's neck, or makes any other movement designed to help his particular problem, while continuing over the fences.

Trotting-Poles with Fences at Bounce Distances

This exercise also helps the rider's position. It is performed over trotting-poles followed by fences at bounce distances about 2.75 m. (9 ft.) apart. (Suitable for 13.2 hh. ponies jumping fences at 60 cm. or 2 ft. high). In this case the distances become even more crucial, as the ponies should land and immediately take off again without a stride. If a long-striding pony tries to jump two fences at a time, or if a short-striding pony takes a stride between the fences, chaos will ensue. Use it, therefore, only when the ponies have worked over trotting-poles, on to gymnastic exercises and are ready to progress. Fig. 42 shows one bounce but further fences may be added, with the same distance between them once the original fence has been performed satisfactorily.

The distances given above are approximate. They will ultimately depend on the size of the ponies, the lengths of their strides, and the height of the fences.

Gymnastics without Trotting-Poles
These have a special value in developing or restoring confidence when jumping from the canter—though they may also be approached from the trot. They are used most effectively when giving a private lesson or a lesson with a small number of riders whose ponies have identical strides. Sometimes a ride may be split into two groups, and the distances adjusted for each group.

Equipment
A minimum of four pairs of stands and nine poles will be needed.

Positioning of Equipment
Build a small fence, and position the stands ready to build two more fences each about 6 m. away from the last. Use two pairs of stands for a third fence. At this stage do not position the stands accurately.

Method
After the ride has carried out the usual preliminary exercises and has jumped the small jump from trot and canter, build a second larger fence 6 m. (approx. 19.5 ft.) away. This distance should be correct for ponies of 13.2 hh. approaching the double in a steady canter. Watch each pony jump the double carefully, and repeat the exercise until the whole ride is jumping it fluently. If necessary, adjust the distance between the fences and repeat the exercise again to check that the adjustment was satisfactory.

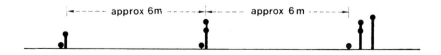

Fig. 43 A combination of three jumps, seen from the side.

Then build a third fence (Fig. 43) the same distance away, but make it a staircase type, and measure to its first pole (the take-off pole). Make it larger than the other two, with the spread the same as the height.

The ride should approach the fence at a steady canter, the first fence being merely a placing fence to help the ponies to arrive correctly at the second fence, which will require more effort. The third-largest fence will need an even higher jump, but the ponies should find it easy, as the previous two fences will have regulated their balance and stride. The riders will learn to sit quietly, maintaining rhythm and impulsion.

If the distances are correct and the ponies are not rushing the approach to the placing fence, the second and third fences may be enlarged. Then, if all is well, the third fence may be raised again. In this way, ponies and riders find themselves approaching a larger fence confidently and without having to worry about arriving at the correct point for the take-off. Beware of over-facing the ponies.

Jumping-Lanes

Jumping-lanes are most useful, but unfortunately they are seldom available. Any of the previous exercises may be used in them. Because they have high fences which run along both sides of the lane, 'steering' problems are minimal.

In jumping-lanes the riders can concentrate on their positions and on the movement of their ponies. Once the riders are performing fluently over easy fences, they can carry out the exercises without reins, stirrups, saddles—or with their eyes closed—according to their ability. Take care that the work without stirrups or saddles does not cause tension and upward gripping with the calves. Do not allow the riders to hold on by the reins.

Warnings

1. Knowledge of distances and careful measuring are poor substitutes for the Coach/Instructor's eyes. While helping the riders, watch the ponies carefully as they negotiate trotting-poles and perform gymnastic exercises. If necessary, adjust the distances, and repeat the exercise with the whole ride. Every inch matters, and because distances are crucial, you must ensure that they are correct for all the ponies at each stage before progressing to the next. If this is not possible, do not continue with gymnastic jumping. If distances are wrong, the value of the exercise is lost, and an accident may well result.
2. Gradients and the state of the going affect distances. A distance which is correct in the indoor school will be far too long in a muddy field or up an incline.
3. Ponies who are tired or bored tend to trip, and may even fall. Jumping must be stopped before this stage is reached.

26 Gaining More from a Session

Many inexperienced Coach/Instructors work the ride one behind the other. This is not helpful for the future, when they are not in a ride at a rally. As soon as possible the riders should work in open order. Even the smallest ride may be able to work on this for a limited period in walk, and by the time the ride is at D+ level most of the work should be in open order.

There are two main methods of working a more senior ride, depending on the numbers and the space available.
1. Riders, on the same rein and well spaced out round the arena, practise the same movement. When a rider feels that he is getting too close to the horse ahead he should make a turn or circle, rejoining the ride in an empty space, without breaking his horse's rhythm. At this stage it is important for each horse to work in a way which is best for him as an individual. When a rider feels that he or his horse are getting tired or have achieved their objective, he should walk his horse on a loose rein, off the track, until he is ready to work again. The Coach/Instructor, while watching all the members of the ride, should give individual help and advice. He or she should remember to change the rein at regular intervals. Later in the lesson, it may be sensible to use all the available space rather than being confined by the markers.
2. When the ride is small in number and the horses are reasonably settled there is no need for all the riders to be on the same rein. As long as there is adequate space and a competent Coach/Instructor they may each work at their own task. They should be reminded to pass oncoming riders left hand to left hand.

Coaches/Instructors should ensure that all riders:
• Are made aware of their own problems and how best to improve themselves.
• Learn to analyse the reasons for what they as individuals are doing.
• Are encouraged to feel and recognise why a movement went wrong and how to improve it.
• Practise putting their thoughts and feelings into words.
• Think towards progressive training for their horses.
• Consider whether improvement might be achieved by changes to the pony/horse's care, i.e. feeding, bedding, care of feet, etc.

27　Working a Rider on the Lunge

Read the current *Manual of Horsemanship*: 'The Position of the Rider in the Saddle' and 'The Position of the Rider in Motion'. Also read 'Lungeing' in *Breeding, Backing and Bringing on Young Horses and Ponies*.

Purpose

To improve the position of the rider. Without the need to control the horse, the rider is able to concentrate on improving his riding. This improvement will help him to be more effective in all branches of horsemanship by:

1. Building his confidence.
2. Improving his balance.
3. Developing a supple, secure and elegant position from which the aids can be correctly and easily applied.
4. Eliminating stiffness.

These will lead to the development of 'feel' and will result in increased harmony between horse and rider.

Standard

Lungeing helps the riders at all levels provided that the Coach/Instructor is sufficiently skilled, and that the length and demands of the lesson are appropriate.

The Coach/Instructor should at all times pay attention to the following:

1. Confidence
2. The rider's balance, especially through transitions and changes of speed. The rider should not tip forwards or backwards and should be aware of the equal distribution of weight on both seat bones.
3. Confidence, suppleness and balance are interdependent. Lack of confidence can create stiffness. Stiffness can disrupt balance.
4. If the rider is struggling to keep his balance, there is no point in the Coach/Instructor telling him to 'relax'. Confidence must first be restored by returning to a slower pace or even to the halt in order to reestablish this essential balance.
5. Evidence of excess tension can be seen in all parts of the body, but it is most clearly revealed in the extremities—i.e. head, hands, and feet.

Requirements

1. A suitable horse or pony who is accustomed to being used for lungeing a rider, and whose paces are regular, steady and comfortable. It is important that he responds to the commands given to him, while ignoring those given, in a different tone, to the rider.
2. A Coach/Instructor or assistant to lunge the horse. Whoever does so must have the necessary experience and knowledge of lungeing to maintain complete control. It can be advantageous for the Coach/Instructor to be free to stand on the outside of the circle so that he or she can observe the rider from all sides.
3. Correct lungeing equipment, including a saddle which fits both horse and rider, and a bridle. *See* 'Lungeing' in *Breeding, Backing and Bringing on Young Horses and Ponies* for correct equipment and how to fit it.
4. A suitable site; preferably an enclosed flat area with good going, approximately 20 to 30 m. square.

Method

1. Before the rider mounts, the horse should be worked at walk, trot and canter on both reins, until he is settled and obedient. It is usual to work first without, and later with, side reins. Secure the side reins to each other over the withers when they are not fastened to the bit.
2. When the horse is ready, bring him to a halt and unfasten the side reins. The rider should mount, adjust the stirrup leathers and take up a loose rein. The bridle reins are there in the first place to give the rider confidence. As soon as the rider is happy, they can be secured over the neck and need not be used again. But they should always be there in case of an emergency.
3. At the halt, show the rider how to rest both hands lightly on the pommel of the saddle; and how easy it is, from there, to slip the fingers under the pommel at any time if he feels insecure. This will be his emergency procedure if he loses his balance later on. HE SHOULD NEVER HOLD ON BY THE REINS.
4. Explain the correct position. Refasten the side reins.
5. At the walk, encourage the rider to feel the movement of the horse. The correct position should be maintained. Check that the rider's hips are parallel with the horse's hips and that his shoulders are parallel with the horse's shoulders.
6. Do some simple loosening exercises which allow the rider to discover the freedom of riding without reins—e.g. arm-circling, one arm at a time.

7. To establish confidence the rider may have a brief period, retaining his stirrups, in rising and then in sitting trot. The easiest trot at this stage is a slow, rather idle, pace, with the horse's head low.
8. The Coach/Instructor must use his discretion in deciding what the next stage will be. With some riders, further work with stirrups will be required. In general, some work without stirrups is beneficial. Depending on the rider's standard and fitness, the lesson may contain a mixture of:
   • Transitions
   • Variations in pace and speed.
   • Exercises.
9. Only advanced riders on experienced lunge-horses should be allowed to canter.
10. Work on the lunge is strenuous and should be broken up by frequent periods of rest and discussion. A total of ten minutes' work may be too much for those unaccustomed to riding a lunged horse.
11. During periods of rest, and at the end of the lesson, encourage the rider to stretch and then shake out any stiffness which has crept into his body.
12. Remember to work equally on both reins.
13. Unfasten the side reins from the bit before the rider dismounts.

NOTE: The Coach/Instructor should be alert to the rider's position at all times, making helpful comments and corrections.

Exercises

These will usually be performed at the walk.

Chapter 8 (page 48) deals with physical exercises. Those described under 'A Few Exercises Used for Specific Purposes' are all suitable for the rider on the lunge. As the rider is not controlling the horse and need not hold the reins, he is free to perform a greater variety of exercises, especially with his upper body. Some of these are:
1. Slowly moving the head, describing with the nose a horizontal figure-of-eight (the sign of infinity).
2. Individual arm-circling, upwards, backwards and round.
3. Both arms circling, as above, or swinging forward and backwards.
4. Position of the hands:
   (a) Holding the saddle.
   (b) Straight down by the horse's sides.
   (c) Arms outstretched sideways, palms uppermost.
   (d) Hands on the head, elbows in line with shoulders.
   (e) Hands in riding position.

5. Arms to the side and circling individually forwards upwards and across, at the same time twisting the trunk to touch the point of the horse's opposite hip with the fingers.
6. Arms to the side and a little to the rear, without body movement, bringing the heels up alternately to touch the hands.
7. Raising one arm then bending down to touch the toe on the same side.
8. Knee and thigh taken sideways off the saddle (short periods only).

Perhaps the most useful exercise to be performed by the rider at the halt or walk is stretching both legs slowly down and a little backward out to the side from the hip joint, then allowing them to return to the saddle, keeping the knees low on the saddle flap. This will help to improve the rider's leg position, with the thigh flat against the saddle.

The Coach/Instructor must decide when the rider is too relaxed or too tense and use suitable exercises to help him. He or she should take care that problems such as upward gripping with the thighs and calves, or tension in other places, do not result from doing work which is too difficult for the rider at that stage. Remember that as the pace increases the same exercises become more difficult.

The More Advanced Rider

He will be able to have a longer lesson but should still have frequent periods of physical rest at the walk, during which discussion may be useful. Only when his position is basically correct will he be able to stay in balance. If for any reason he becomes insecure and is unable to regain his balance, the horse should be brought back to walk.

Riders working for the 'A' test should be able to maintain a supple and independent position on the lunge, with the hands in the riding position.

Working a rider on the lunge

Appendix

The Pony Club Test standards have been written to provide a continuous ladder of learning for all riders. The knowledge required for each test underpins the knowledge required for the next.

The ages at which the test may be taken are an indication at what age the work may be suitable, but they are not written in stone and many members will benefit from work above or below the ages suggested on the cards. Care, however should be taken to ensure any underpinning knowledge is in place before moving on to new work.

The movements and understanding asked for at each level are equally applicable for the member who wishes to do no more than enjoy their pony, or the keen competition rider. It is the challenge to the Coach/Instructor to enable the rider to know how the work will benefit that individual.

The tests also provide a training route for the ponies and horses, so the education of the youngsters is less haphazard.

Pony Club Standards of Efficiency

The Efficiency Tests provide a staircase of knowledge and progression when taken in sequence.

'E' STANDARD—TEST SHEET 2007

This is an official voluntary test for young new Members. It is not necessary to either take or pass the Test before attempting the D Test. Candidates should be accompanied by an instructor. The test may be taken on or off the lead rein.

Objective

To improve and enjoy learning about ponies.
To be happy both on and around ponies
To know the basic points of the pony.

Riding

To be able to sit on a pony in halt and at walk.

To be able to hold the reins.

With help, carry out physical exercises such as:

- Touch parts of the pony, mane, neck, tail, etc.
- To be to able to ride the pony away from the examiner at walk, turn round a cone and go back to the examiner.
- To be able to show trot (rising is not necessary) on the leading rein.
- To be able to stop at a designated point and say 'thank you'.

Horsemastership

(Must be accompanied by an adult helper).

To know the name and colour of the pony they are riding.

To recognise:

- Saddle
- Bridle
- Mane
- Tail
- Ears
- Eyes
- Mouth
- Legs
- Hooves

To be able to feed the pony a carrot correctly.

Look at/Read:

Pony Club Sticker Books 1, 2 and 3
Colour and Learn
Native Ponies Colouring Book
Trace, Copy and Colour
Pony Guide File

To Be Followed by: The Pony Club Bronze Award 3, 2, and 1
Felt Colour: Pale Yellow

'D' STANDARD—TEST SHEET 2010

The Road Rider Mini Achievement Badge is a prerequisite before taking the 'D' Test.

Objective

To have a basic understanding of ponies.
To achieve confidence in handling and riding a pony.
To improve and enjoy learning about ponies.
To hold more Mini Achievement Badges.

Riding

Mount and dismount.
Understand and show a correct position in the saddle at halt.
Be able to hold the reins correctly.
Be able to ride a quiet pony safely, in an enclosed area without the
  leading rein, in walk and trot.

Pony Care

Approach and handle a pony correctly.
Know basic needs of a pony in summer and winter.
Catch a pony and put on a headcollar.
Proper way to give a pony an apple or carrot.
Lead a pony in hand in walk and turn correctly.
Tie up correctly.
Name simple points of the pony.
Name different parts of saddle and bridle.
Recognise a dandy brush and rubber curry comb.

Read

Keeping a Pony at Grass
The Manual of Horsemanship—study the sections below:
• Points of the horse
• Mount and dismount (Omit 'to dismount using the stirrup')
• The correct length of stirrup leather
• The position of the rider in the saddle
• Holding single reins
• Handling a horse
• Fitting a headcollar
• Leading and showing in hand
• The parts of a saddle
• The parts of a snaffle bridle
• Putting on a saddle and bridle

View (DVDs)
Stable Management series: *Handling and Leading*
                                         Health and Condition

Recommended Minimum Age: 8 years
Felt Colour: Yellow

'D+' STANDARD—TEST SHEET 2010
This is a Test half way between 'D' and 'C'.

Objective
To be working towards developing a balanced seat independent of the reins.

Riding
Mount and dismount.
Know how to alter stirrups correctly when mounted.
Know how to check girths.
Sit correctly at the walk and be able to describe the correct position.
Hold the reins correctly and carry a whip in either hand.
Walk on a loose rein and shorten the reins.
Begin to demonstrate a balanced seat in trot and canter.
Count their pony's rhythm in trot.
Correct use of legs as aids.
Simple turns and circles in walk and trot.
Rising trot on either diagonal, change of diagonal.
Show a few strides of sitting trot through transitions.
Walk without stirrups.
Ride up and down hills in walk.
Ride over a single pole and very small fence.
To be able to control a quiet pony in company, on the roads and
   in the countryside.

What You Need to Know
(This is likely to relate to the horse or pony being ridden.)
To understand and describe the aids to halt, walk,trot,canter, and
circles, and be able to apply them.
Give a simple definition of a pony working forwards.
Be able to explain rhythm—evenness and regularity in trot.

Pony Care

To have some knowledge of care and working a pony at grass.
Put on a saddle, bridle and numnah (snaffle bridle only).
Have some knowledge of correctly fitting tack (noseband, throat lash, numnah).
Elementary care of saddlery (daily bit washing, importance of clean girths, numnahs and saddle cloths).
Catch a pony and turn him out in a field.
Lead a pony in hand at walk and trot and turn correctly.
Names and uses of essential grooming kit.
Show how to use a dandy brush.
Pick up and pick out feet.
Points of the pony, colours and markings.
Be able to recognise stable rugs, turn out rugs, and rugs suitable for travel and hot sweaty ponies.

Read

Pony Guide File
Keeping a Pony at Grass
Games, Gags and Guesses
Tricky Tests and Teasers
Posers and Puzzles
The Manual of Horsemanship —study the sections below:
• Points of the Pony
• Colours and markings
• Care and working a pony off grass
• Putting on a saddle
• Putting on a bridle
• Unsaddling
• Saddle fitting
• Bridle fitting
• To tie up correctly
• Care of Saddlery
• Grooming
• Aids (Omit gallop and rein-back)
• Jumping position
• Points of the Horse

View (DVDs)

Road Rider
Stable Management series: *Handling and Leading*
                             Health and Condition

Recommended Minimum Age: 10 years
Felt Colour: White

'C' STANDARD—TEST SHEET 2010

Before being awarded the 'C' Test Certificate, Candidates must have trained for and passed The Pony Club's Road Rider Achievement Badge or The Pony Club Road Rider Test or the BHS Riding and Road Safety Test.

Objective

To understand the importance of, and to be working towards
  a secure correct balanced seat, independent of the reins.
To understand why a correct seat is important.
To apply simple aids correctly.
To have a knowledge of the care and working of a pony off grass.
To be in control of the pony on the roads and in the countryside.
To have a proper regard for country lore.

Riding

Turn-out of pony and rider.
Mount and dismount correctly on either side.
Hold the reins correctly.
Alter stirrups when mounted.
Tighten and loosen girth when mounted.
Working towards a balanced, independent seat.
Use of seat, legs and hands as aids to increase and decrease pace.
Ride without stirrups in walk and trot—as long as it is safe.
Sitting trot, rising trot on the correct diagonal and change of diagonal.
Understand the meaning of, and start to establish, the pony's rhythm.
Walk with a long rein.
Canter on both reins.
Riding school drill.
Ride up and down hill in walk and trot.
Independent work in the open.
Walk and trot over heavy poles as a preliminary to jumping.
Ride in a balanced position over small fences.
Show a smooth progression from one fence to the next.
Riding in the countryside, across farm land and bridle paths.
Open and close gates.

What You Need to Know
(This is likely to relate to the horse or pony being ridden.)
Know simple aids and ride turns and circles at walk, trot and canter.
Aids for canter on a named leg on a circle.
Explain sequence of legs in trot and canter.
Understand the meaning of rhythm and tempo.

Horse and Pony Care
Care and working of a pony off grass.
Elementary feeding, watering and cleanliness of the pony.
Groom a grass kept pony.
Put on a tail bandage.
Know when a pony needs shoeing.
Put on a saddle, bridle and martingale.
Have some knowledge of correctly fitting tack (saddle clearing
   withers, height of bit).
Be able to do up a curb chain correctly.
Know correct fitting for a flash nose band.
Elementary care and cleaning of saddlery (tack care after daily exercise).
Know the main indications for health in the pony.
Know how to clean minor wound.
Know which wounds require veterinary attention.
Understand the reason for anti-tetanus vaccination and know
   when their pony was vaccinated.
Recognise when a pony is clearly lame.
Know how to take a pony in and out of a horse-box or trailer
   with adult supervision.
Understand the importance and the means of protecting the legs
   while travelling.
Put on and take off, stable and turn out rugs.

Read
Keeping a Pony at Grass
Pony Guide File
The Manual of Horsemanship—study the sections below:
• Mounting and dismounting (Omit 'to dismount using the stirrup')
• The stirrups
• The position of the rider in the saddle
• Holding the single rein
• Position of the rider in motion
• The aids
• The basic paces (Omit 'the rein back')

- Jumping
- The correct approach
- Identification and Classification
- Saddling up
- Putting on and fitting a bridle, unsaddling
- Care of saddlery
- The signs of good health
- Lameness—identifying the lame leg
- Loading—with an assistant
- Unloading

The Country Code—The Countryside Commission
Wallcharts: *Tack, Grooming, Native Ponies, First Aid*

View (DVDs)
Road Rider

Recommended Minimum Age: 11 years
Felt Colour: Green

'C+' STANDARD—TEST SHEET 2010

Before taking the 'C+' Test, candidates must have passed the 'C' Test, including the Road Rider Achievement Badge. Riders may be required to change horses or ponies for some flat work.

To become an educated and practical rider.
To ride over fences at all paces.
To gain practical experience and knowledge of the care of
  a stabled pony and of a pony at grass.
To be capable of riding a well-mannered pony out hunting and
  in all Pony Club activities.
To ride intelligently and with due regard for others on the roads
  and in the country, and with a knowledge of pace, distance and
  discipline when riding alone and in groups.

Riding
Working towards a supple, balanced position on the flat and over fences.
Comment on the suppleness of rider's own horse.
Discuss horses' response to the aids and any loss of balance.
Apply aids correctly for increase and decrease of pace, turns and circles.
Turns on the forehand from the halt.

Stand still. Salute.
Free walk on a long rein or with a loose rein.
Change of leg at canter through trot and talk about balance of the horse.
Know the aids for and show leg yielding at walk.
Ride with reins in one hand.
Ride up and down steep hills and banks.
Jump a variety of fences show jumping and cross country.
Jump up and down hill.
Identify which fence was jumped the best and why.
Jump doubles.

What You Need to Know
(This is likely to relate to the horse or pony being ridden.)
Understand the reasons for the equipment the horse or pony is wearing.
Discuss the advantages of a correct position.
Name the Scales of Training.
Discuss whether the horse or pony is working forwards in
    a suitable rhythm and tempo.
Understand the meaning of suppleness in a horse or pony.
Know the sequence of legs at all paces.

Horse and Pony Care
Practical care and working of a pony off grass.
Knowledge of the care, feed and work of a stabled pony.
Know principles of watering and feeding.
Have knowledge of the different items of forage.
Understand the importance of roughage.
Recognise when to feed hay or haylage.
Know the articles of grooming kit and be able to use them effectively.
Know the structure of the horse's foot as shown in the Manual.
Know the names of the farrier's tools.
Be able to name external parts of the foot.
Describe a hunter shoe.
Be able to fit a saddle and bridle.
Bits and their uses; snaffle, double jointed snaffles and the action of gags.
Prepare a horse for travel.
Load and unload safely.
Put on a stable bandage.
Know when a horse is lame.
Identify signs of illness.
Know the symptoms and reason for poor condition.

Know when to call the vet.
Be able to care for a wound until vet arrives.
Be able to put a poultice on a leg.

Read
The Manual of Horsemanship
Keeping a Pony at Grass
The Country Code—The Countryside Commission
Pony Guide File
Achievement Badge Buddies: *Lorinery, Cleaning Tack*
Equipment Safety Achievement Badge Syllabus

View (DVDs)
Road Rider
Stable Management series: *Handling and Leading*
  Health and Condition

Recommended Minimum Age: 13 years
Felt Colour: Pink

ROAD RIDER TEST—TEST SHEET 2010

Aim
The aim of the Road Rider Test is to promote safety on the road by recognising riders who can show that they ride with courtesy and responsibility, are aware of and obey the law, the *Highway Code* and the *Road Rider* book and the British Horse Society's *Riding and Road Craft Manual*.

To be taken at 'C+' to 'B' Test Level. Members should attain this level before going on to take their 'B' Test. Those wishing to take their British Horse Society Stages will need to achieve the British Horse Society's Riding and Road Safety Test. For details of the BHS test contact the BHS Safety Office.

Details of the training, running, organisation and administration of The Pony Club Road Rider Test can be found on the Pony Club website.

Riders must be over 12 years old and should have been well prepared by working up the three Pony Club Road Rider test levels:
• The Pony Club Road Rider Mini Achievement Badge (E/D Test)
• The Pony Club Road Rider Achievement Badge (D+/C Test)
• The Pony Club Road Rider Test (C+/B Test)

Examination Panel for the Pony Club Road Rider Test

Riding Examiner   A Pony Club 'C' Test Examiner or above
                          who is also an experienced driver.
Road Safety Examiner   A Pony Club examiner who has studied
                          the *Road Rider* DVD and *Junior Road Rider*
                          book and is also an experienced driver.

The Test

The Test is of the rider's road craft and riding ability and not of the horse
or pony. NB. There is no such thing as a bomb-proof horse or pony.

Test candidates are required to take the test in three parts consecutively.

Members should have achieved the previous level and be able to
demonstrate understanding of the following sections:

Theory Test

Designed to test the rider's knowledge of the *Highway Code* and of the
generally accepted rules of riding on the highway as set out in the
current edition of *Junior Road Rider*. Ten questions may be given
orally or in the form of a test paper and should invite factual answers,
not opinions. Recommended sample questions are given on the
website. Candidates should achieve 8 out of 10 to pass this section.

Tack And Turnout Inspection

This inspection is entirely a safety measure carried out to make sure
that the horse's tack and rider's clothing are in a safe and satisfactory
condition for riding. It is not a 'show' inspection. Hats must be to the
current BSI Standard(s) and properly secured.

Members Should Be Able to Demonstrate:

1. Dress accordingly for the road (horse and rider).
2. Know the importance of Be Seen to Be Safe.
3. Necessary checks before going on the road.
4. Recognition of common road signs.
5. Understand the sequence of traffic lights and the meaning of the
   amber light and how to behave at traffic lights.
6. Be able to explain what position a rider should take when
   negotiating a roundabout.

Complex Simulated Route

Designed to test in safe but simulated road conditions, a rider's precautions against and reactions to a series of noises and sights which reasonably could be met with locally on the roads and which might make a horse shy.

Road junctions must be included so that candidates may demonstrate their road craft and ability to use arm signals. Hazards must be placed far enough apart to allow candidates to show TROT between each or any of them. **Trot must be shown** by candidates at this stage of the test.

To Be Ridden as a Complete Route:
• Major to minor and minor to major.
• Two left turns and two right turns.
• A stop and give way sign, hazards and trot.
• Observation, road positioning and signals.
• Correct sequence for making a left or right signal.
• Look—signal—look again ('life saver look')—manoeuvre.
• How to say 'Thank you'.

Marking

To be successful the candidate must pass in all three parts of the test. A candidate who fails in either part one or part two may not take part three. The test is of the rider not of the horse. To be successful the candidate must satisfy the examiners in all three parts of the test consecutively. Eight out of ten theory questions must be correctly answered. A Test Marking Sheet can be found on the website together with Notes for Examiners. Any manoeuvre which is judged as dangerous to other road users could result in failure.

Essential Reading

The Pony Club Junior Road Rider book and Road Rider DVD
Tales of the Road—A highway code for young road users
The British Horse Society's *Riding and Road Craft Manual*
The *Highway Code*—current edition available from TSO
Certificates and badges available from The Pony Club.

Caution The Pony Club recommend that young riders who have passed the Road Rider Safety Test should be encouraged to take the BHS Road Safety Test before riding on the road unaccompanied and even then only when the person responsible for their safety is entirely satisfied that, in their opinion, it is safe for the young person(s) to do so.

'B' STANDARD—TEST SHEET 2010

The Test may be taken as a whole or in two parts:
• B Standard Horse and Pony Care
• B Standard Riding

These Tests may be taken on different occasions and in any order.

Before taking the 'B' Test, Candidates must have passed the 'C+' Test and The Pony Club Road Rider Test or the BHS Riding and Road Safety Test.

Bringing pressure to bear on Area Representatives, DCs, Examiners and other Pony Club Officials to treat as special cases those who happen to be using the Test as an Entry/Professional Qualification is unacceptable.

'B' STANDARD HORSE AND PONY CARE

Objective
To gain practical experience and knowledge of the care of a stabled horse/pony and of a horse/pony at grass.

To look after these before, during and after the day's hunting, eventing or endurance.

Horse and Pony Care
Knowledge of the care and working of a pony at grass and a stabled horse receiving hard feed.

A fittening routine suitable for Intermediate/Open Area Pony Club competitions.

The importance of exercise for stable kept horses.

Daily routine for grass kept and stabled horses.

Have some knowledge of stabling—ventilation, light, drainage, shelter and warmth.

Know principles of watering and feeding and why these principles are important.

Have a knowledge of the different items of forage, and their effect on a horse's condition and behaviour.

Put on a stable bandage.

Discuss types of rug, tail and poll guards, etc.

Inspect horse box or trailer for safety and road-worthiness.

Recognise good and bad points of conformation.

Know the parts of the horse's shoe and different types of shoe.

Understand the methods of shoeing.

Know uses of the farrier's tools.

Know when a horse is in healthy condition.

Know how to administer a wormer.

Know when a horse is lame or ill and discuss the most likely causes of these ailments.

Elementary first aid including colic, laminitis and azoturia/tying up.

Explain how to take a temperature.

Discuss how to administer medicine in food, tub a foot, hose a leg and put a poultice on a foot.

Organisation and fitting of tack room.

Understand and discuss the families of bitting, characteristics, action and probable reaction.

Recognise badly fitting tack and inspect tack for soundness.

Know how to store saddlery, rugs , bandages, etc.

Recognition of various types of saddles, martingales and boots and their uses.

Read

The Manual of Horsemanship
Keeping a Pony at Grass
Young Persons Guide to Eventing
The Scales of Training
Stablemates series: *(1) Vital Statistics*
                        (2) Body Basics
                        (3) Fit for the Bit
Wallcharts: *Respiratory System, Digestive System, Points and Skeleton of the Horse, Areas of Common Ailments and Injuries, Poisonous Plants, First Aid, Lorinery*

Suggested Further Reading

Pasture Management

View (DVDs)

Stable Management series: *Handling and Leading*
                              Health and Condition

Only those 14 years or over are eligible for 'B' Standard.
Recommended Minimum Age: 15 years
Felt Colour: Red (Both sections of 'B' Test)
                                 Brown (Horse & Pony Care
                                      section only)

'B' STANDARD RIDING

Objective
To become an effective rider who knows the reasons for what he or she
   is doing.
To know the Scales of Training.
To understand the Scales provide a staircase of training suitable for all
   horses and ponies.
To be able to maintain a horse's way of going.
To ride over fences at all paces.
To be capable of riding a well-mannered horse or pony out hunting, in
   horse trials, or on a long distance ride.
To ride intelligently and with due regard for others in the country, with a
   knowledge of pace, distance and discipline when riding alone and in groups.

Riding
Basically correct position at walk, trot, canter, gallop and over fences.
Try a horse at his basic paces, transitions, turns and circles.
Understand and apply the correct aids for the movements ridden during
   this Test.
Understand the aids for, and be able to ride, lengthened strides, rein
   back and leg yielding in walk and trot.
Work towards demi pirouette in walk.
Halt and salute.
Candidates may be asked to ride with two pairs of reins and should
   understand the influence of the two reins.
School movements, including work without stirrups.
Ride a show jumping course and assess the round.
Ride up and down hills and banks in trot and canter.
Jump a variety of cross country fences while maintaining rhythm and a
   balanced position.
Jump up and down hill; jump drop fences, jump doubles and awkward fences.
Show a knowledge of pace and balance suitable for the level of training
   and fitness of their horse whilst riding at a cross-country speed.

What You Need to Know
(This is likely to relate to the horse or pony being ridden.)
Having tried a horse at his basic paces, transitions, turns and circles,
   comment on findings using the Scales of Training as a template.
Analyse the horse's rhythm, tempo and suppleness.
Understand the meaning of contact, impulsion, and straightness.

Discuss the balance of the horse.

Know the distances of trotting-poles, a placing pole to a fence and a one stride double of 90 cm. high.

Read
The Manual of Horsemanship
Young Persons Guide to Eventing
Young Persons Guide to Show Jumping
To Be A Dressage Rider
Endurance Riding and Trekking
Stablemates series: *(3) Fit for the Bit*

Suggested Further Reading
Rule Books for Pony Club Dressage, Show Jumping and Eventing
The Scales of Training
Wallcharts: *The Muscular System, Points and Skeleton of the Horse*

Only those 14 years or over are eligible for 'B' Standard.

Recommended Minimum Age:	15 years
Felt Colour:	Red—Both sections of 'B' Test
	Beige—Riding Section only

LUNGEING TEST—TEST SHEET 2010

General
Before taking the Lungeing Test, Candidates must have passed the 'B' Test or 'B' Standard Horse and Pony Care.

It is necessary to pass the Lungeing Test before attempting the AH Test. This Test is examined by an AH Examiner.

Objective
To be able to work the horse for exercise on the lunge.

Requirements
Enclosed lunge area
Lunge horse
Equipment
(Candidates may lunge their own horse or one provided by the test organiser.)

Lunge area: Check for safety, enclosed clear space with non-slip surface.
Equipment: Check the required equipment to include lunge rein
and whip, hat, gloves and safe footwear. Horse will
have been previously groomed in preparation for work.
Fit saddle...   ...with breastplate, girth and stirrups correctly
secured.
Fit lunge cavesson: Check size, fit straps under bridle tight enough to
prevent slipping but without pressure on the soft
part of the nose or cheekbones.
Fit bridle: Remove noseband and secure reins in throat lash.
Fit side reins: Adjust side reins to the correct height and length so
as not to inhibit the horse and clip back to D rings
whilst the horse is warmed up.
Fit boots: Brushing and overreach boots.
Lunge a well-behaved horse or pony: Handling equipment safely,
correctly and effectively.
Use clear commands, stand in a safe position.
Use an appropriate-sized circle and include changes of rein.
Work for a suitable rhythm using appropriate exercises.
Show sensible use of side reins.
The horse should be lunged for a sufficient length of time
to show active exercise which will maintain health.
Cooling-Off: Side reins undone, allow horse to stretch at end of work.
Be able to discuss quality of work shown, recognising
the correct or incorrect way of going, including rhythm
and suppleness of the horse.

Read
Breeding, Backing and Bringing on Young Horses and Ponies

View DVDs
Stable Management series: *Handling and Leading*
Health and Condition

Recommended Minimum Age: 16 years
Felt Colour: Light blue

COACHING CERTIFICATE—TEST SHEET 2010

General
Before taking the Coaching Certificate, Candidates must have passed the 'B' Test. It is recommended that Candidates should have attended the Year 1 and Year 2 Pony Club 'Introduction to Coaching' Courses and attend First Aid and Child Protection Training.

Objective
To give candidates a sound base of coaching knowledge, to enable them to teach a group of riders up to 'C' standard and a group of 'C+' standard for horse care.

Safety
Risk assessment and practical solution to hazards found.
Understand safety procedures involved in planning a hack.
Understand safety procedures involved in organising a ridden or dismounted lesson.
Check the fitting and suitability of tack of their pupils.
Assess riders and situation throughout the riding session to ensure safety.
Know correct procedures in event of an accident
Fill in an accident form.

Riding Session
Plan and teach a one hour lesson up to 'C' Test level for a group of between four and six riders, to include jumping. Candidates must also supervise riders until they are in the care of their parents and/or guardians.
Teach a lead rein lesson.

Coaching Skills Required
An audible and well-modulated voice.
Ability to communicate.
Wear correct clothing, clean, tidy and fit for purpose.
Know and use school commands.
Demonstrate the ability to improve the horsemanship of their pupils.
Describe a progressive plan for their pupils' next lesson, setting short and long-term goals.

Horse Care Session
Produce and be able to discuss plans for two thirty minute horse/pony care sessions, one for 'D'+ and one for 'C+'.
Teach a thirty minute horse/pony care session up to 'C+' level.

Read

The Manual of Horsemanship
The Instructors Handbook
Young Persons Guide to Eventing
Young Persons Guide to Show Jumping
To Be A Dressage Rider
The Scale of Training (from the Pony Club website: www.pcuk.org)
UKCC Learning Resource Pack (the Pony Club website: www.pcuk.org)
Stablemates series: *(1) Vital Statistics*
                        (2) Body Basics
                        (3) Fit for the Bit

Recommended Minimum Age: 18 years

'AH' STANDARD—TEST SHEET 2010

General

The Pony Club 'AH' Test stands alone as the highest Test of
horsemastership available in the Pony Club. It is a prerequisite for the
'A' Test Riding, replacing the Horsemastership section of that Test.

It is recommended that where possible, candidates should take the
two tests within a year of each other. Applicants for 'A' Test Riding
need not hold 'AH' at the time of nomination, but will be required to
give the date on which it is intended to take 'AH'. They will not be
allowed to do the 'A' Test Riding unless already successful at 'AH'.
Candidates must be at least 16 years, but 17 years is advised, and must
hold the 'B' Test Certificate and have attained the Lungeing Test before
applying for the 'AH' Test. Those Candidates who have only attained
'C+' Test Horse and Pony Care and the Lungeing Test will be allowed
to attempt 'AH' subject to a satisfactory riding assessment carried out
by an 'AH' Test Examiner appointed by the Area Representative.

The Test may not be attempted on more than three occasions
without further assessment by an 'AH' Test Examiner.

Candidates should be thoroughly familiar with all practical
requirements of the Test so that they are able to carry them out with
speed and efficiency even under examination conditions. It is
important to work in a yard for a time beforehand, handling strange
horses under all conditions and keeping to routine. In addition,

veterinary surgeons and farriers are often willing to take interested and responsible candidates on their rounds, which provide invaluable experience. Candidates should try to read widely, as methods of feeding and veterinary treatment, in particular, are constantly changing and developing. Whilst having a firm grasp of traditional methods, they should be able to discuss modern thinking on these subjects, particularly, and have seen them in practice.

Candidates are expected to show common sense, be forward thinking, confident and positive in all they do. Tasks should be carried out in a safe, efficient, effective and practical way.

Remember:
1. Only wear gloves when actually lungeing, riding or leading a horse. Do not tack up or bandage with them on; it will make you slow and fumbly.
2. When checking tack be methodical, look at both sides and only do it once.
3. Always untie the horse when looking at his teeth.
4. Always hang up the headcollar, or remove it from box if the horse is not wearing it.
5. Always close doors, skip out and pick out feet
6. Always give quantities of food in pounds or kilos, not scoops!
7. To check all tack on horses.

Syllabus and Timetable
Candidates may be examined individually for half a day or in pairs all day at the discretion of the Organiser.

For Four Examiners and Eight Candidates
08.30 am	Briefing and Examiners to check equipment
09.00 am	Start—each section 40 minutes
12.00 pm	Lunch
13.00 pm	Restart
16.00 pm	Confer and talk to candidates.

For Four Examiners and Four Candidates (half a day)
08.30 am	Briefing
09.00 am	Start—four Candidates and four Examiners
12.00 pm	Confer and talk to Candidates and lunch
13.30 pm	Four Candidates and four Examiners
16.30 pm	Confer and talk to candidates

TIME	EXAMINER A	EXAMINER B	EXAMINER C	EXAMINER D
0900	1 & 2	3 & 4	5 & 6	7 & 8
0945	3 & 4	5 & 6	7 & 8	1 & 2
1030	5 & 6	7 & 8	1 & 2	3 & 4
1115	7 & 8	1 & 2	3 & 4	5 & 6
1200	LUNCH—EXAMINERS CONFER			
1300	1 & 2	3 & 4	5 & 6	7 & 8
1345	3 & 4	5 & 6	7 & 8	1 & 2
1430	5 & 6	7 & 8	1 & 2	3 & 4
1515	7 & 8	1 & 2	3 & 4	5 & 6
1600	EXAMINERS CONFER, RESULTS AND TALK TO CANDIDATES			

EXAMINER A—PART 1

Requirements
Two horses tacked up
Saddles
Two snaffle bridles
Breastplates
Boots
Rugs

Tacking-up—Ride and Lead—Leg-Up
A1.   Take two horses out of the stables; mount, ride and lead unaided using snaffle bridles. Lead horse may be tied up outside. *Highway Code.*
A2.   'Put up' person on a horse by giving a leg-up.
A3.   Know how to check tack, hold horse's head and off-side stirrup leather to balance weight of rider mounting.

EXAMINER A—PART 2

Requirements
One horse in stable yard
Well equipped tack room
Shoeing tools and shoes
Grooming kit
Plaiting box
Clippers

Stable Yard
A4. Planning a stable yard, boxes, buildings, light, ventilation, water supply and systems.
A5. Types of bedding, advantages and disadvantages. Siting, building and disposal of muck heap.
A6. Precautions to be taken against fire and burglary.

Foot and Shoeing
A7. Structure of horse's foot.
A8. Recognition of well-shaped and well-shod foot. Faults to look for.
A9. Notice unusual shoeing, pads, etc., wear of shoes and relate to possible unsoundness or movement.
A10. Use of various types of shoe to correct interference, brushing, over-reaching, etc.
A11. Use of studs.
A12. Show how to remove a loose shoe. Tools to use, either farrier's or substitutes if these are not available.
A13. Diseases and ailments related to the foot.

Grooming
A14. Stabled horses and ponies.
A15. Reasons and methods for washing and drying grooming kit and stable equipment.
A16. Reasons for strapping and demonstrate using a leather pad, etc.
A17. How to wash a horse's sheath, mane and tail.
A18. Cooling off a horse after work, including washing down and drying off a wet or sweating horse.

Clipping, Trimming and Plaiting
A19. How to pull or thin manes and tails.
A20. Show how to trim the horse's legs and heels.

A21. How to plait manes and tails.
A22. How to clip. Preparation of: horses, person clipping, stable, safety measures.
A23. Care of clippers; before, during and after clipping.
A24. Types of clip and their uses. Marking horse for clipping.
A25. Dealing with nervous or difficult horses.

Tack Room
A26. Insurance. Accident books and forms.
A27. First aid for riders.
A. Recognition of various normal types of bit and saddlery, their uses, advantages and disadvantages, actions.

EXAMINER B—PART 1

Requirements
Lunge area
Lunge horse (tacked up)
Equipment
Lungeing

B1.   Working the fit horse for exercise on the lunge in a safe, efficient, effective and practical way

---

EXAMINER B—PART 2

Requirements
One horse in stable
A paddock

Paddock Management
B2.   Avoiding worm infestation by regular picking up of droppings and topping rough patches, resting paddock or grazing with sheep or cattle.
B3.   Checking for poisonous plants, shrubs or trees.
B4.   Precautions necessary during and after use of sprays, fertilisers, lime, etc.

Mares and Foals
B5.   Candidates are expected to know the principles of the care of brood mares and the handling of foals and young stock.

Examiners will probably ask Candidates about the following:

Selection of brood mare and of stallion.

Choice of service date—basic outline of covering programme.

Foaling environments, facilities and equipment; selection, preparations and procedures.

Care of the in-foal mare, including feeding, worming and testing routines.

Precautionary measures, e.g. tetanus and influenza.

Signs of mare about to foal.

What to watch out for when mare is foaling.

Deciding factors on whether to return mare to stud; procedures then necessary.

Travelling mares and foals.

Weaning; when and how.

Gelding colts; advantages and disadvantages.

Care of young stock.

How to cope with basic problems which may arise at any time with mares, foals or young stock and know when to call the veterinary surgeon.

EXAMINER C—PART 1

Requirements
A horse in a stable
A flat hard trot-up area
A snaffle bridle

Conformation
C1. Describe a horse fully, including sex, colour, size, age, markings, type and work suited to.
C2. Horseman-like terms or equivalent terms.
C3. Have knowledge of vetting horses for purchase.
C4. Societies and associations connected with the care of horses and ponies.

Health and Condition
C5. What to look for when inspecting the horses first thing in the morning and last thing at night.
C6. Getting a tired horse to stale. Recognising and dealing with symptoms of exhaustion, stress or dehydration after competition or hunting.
C7. The urinary system as related to practical problems.
C8. Taking a temperature

Lameness

C9. Running a horse up for veterinary inspection and comment on action.
C10. How to detect lameness.
C11. Detection of heat and swelling in the horse's leg.
C12. Seats of lameness. Splints, curbs, spavins, etc. Where to find them, what they are, causes and treatments.
C13. Recognition and treatment of diseases and ailments of the foot

---

EXAMINER C—PART 2

Requirements

One horse in stable
Feed room with adequate feed samples
Hay barn if possible.

Feeding

C14. Recognition of good and poor condition and reasons for them.
C15. Rules of watering and feeding and the digestive system.
C16. Organisation of feedstore; rodent control.
C17. Hay and alternatives—horsehage, haylage, etc. Type, qualities, purchasing, storage, quantities to be fed.
C18. Recognition of basic traditional feedstuffs. Knowledge of coarse mixes, nuts, micronised and cooked feedstuffs. Advantages; disadvantages; constituents—carbohydrates, proteins, fats, oils, minerals, vitamins. Quality, quantities to be fed.
C19. Preparation of boiled feeds and reasons for using.
C20. Reasons for use of minerals, additives and probiotics
C21. Green fodder and succulents.
C22. Tempting a difficult feeder, relating to a young , old or sick horse.

Exercise and Fitness

C23. Work and feed when changing horse from one job to another or rest during the year.
C24. Getting a horse fit for competition. Interval training—distance and speed.
C25. Understand the use of horse-walkers.
C26. Relation of feeding to work and condition.
C27. Basic knowledge of the skeletal and muscular systems and their effect on performance and movement.
C28. The lymphatic, and endocrine systems as they relate to practical problems, such as lymphangitis.

C29. Respiratory system, relating to fitness.

C30. Unsoundness of the respiratory system. Whistling, roaring, broken wind, allergies and how to cope with them.

EXAMINER D—PART 1

Requirements
Two horses in two stables
Tack for cross-country
Boots
Exercise bandages

Handling
D1. How to approach, tie up, move about and handle a horse in a stable, and the importance of good stable manners for the horse.
D2. How to hold a horse for treatment.
D3. Handling difficult horses in and out of stables. Use of a twitch.
D4. Dealing with a cast horse in the box, during and after.
D5. Care of horses' teeth. How to examine for sharp or wolf teeth.
D6. Basic knowledge of the nervous system relating to the sensory systems.

Tacking-Up
D7. Types and uses of bandages, materials, alternatives to Gamgee.
D8. Putting on an exercise bandage, boots and tack a horse up for cross-country schooling.
D9. Fit a saddle and a double bridle.

EXAMINER D—PART 2

Requirements
One horse in stable
Access to first aid equipment
Bandages.

Common Ailments—Nursing—First Aid
D10. Recognition of good and ill health.
D11. Simple medical and veterinary terms.
D12. Precautions against infection and contagion. The horse's skin.
D13. Sick nursing.

D14. Understand support and current veterinary bandaging.
D15. Treatment of saddle sores and galls.
D16. Fomenting, tubbing, hosing.
D17. Hot and cold poultices, types and uses; applying to foot.
D18. How to deal with severe bleeding, circulatory system.
D19. Inoculations—types and timing.
D20. Precautions against flies and around stables.
D21. Treatment of coughs, colds, flu and strangles.
D22. Colic; recognition and treatment until vet arrives.
D23. Treatment for all kinds of worms.
D24. Ailments relating to feeding; laminitis, azoturia.
D25. Skin diseases.
D26. Eye diseases.
D27. Wounds—different types and treatment.
   When to call the vet for stitching or advice.

Read
T*he Manual of Horsemanship*
Breeding, Backing and Bringing on Young Horses and Ponies
Endurance Riding and Trekking
USPC Guide to Lungeing and Ground Training
A Working Notebook of a Test Horse and Pony Care
(available from Mrs. Adams Tel: 01284 830098)
Stablemates series: *(1) Vital Statistics*
                       (2) Body Basics
Pasture Management

Suggested Further Reading
Veterinary Notes for the Horse Owner—Hayes
Horse *and Stable Management—*
      J. Houghton Brown and Vincent Powell-Smith
Horse Nutrition and Feeding—Sarah Pilliner
Breeding— pamphlet obtainable from The Ponies UK
Mares, Foals and Foaling—Fredrick Andrist
Horsemaster's Notebook—Mary Rose
Equine Nutrition—Derek Cuddeford
The Horse Shoeing Book—Martin Humphrey
The Complete Equine Veterinary Manual—T. & M. Pavord
Lungeing and Long Reining—Jennie Loriston-Clarke

All publications are available to order from your local library.

View
Pony Club Training Videos:
> *When to Call the Vet*
> *Handling and Leading*
> *Health and Condition*

CD Rom
Under the Horse's Skin—
> available from the British Horse Society *www.bhs.org.uk*

'A' STANDARD—TEST SHEET 2010

Standard Required
Passing the 'A' Test is a worthwhile achievement. It is accepted by the BHS as an exemption from their Stages 3 and 4 Examinations in Riding and Horse Care, (subject to recommendation by The Pony Club Training Committee and approval by the BHS Qualifications and Training Committee).

The 'A' Test is the highest award of The Pony Club, and provides a comprehensive assessment of Horsemanship and Training of Young Horses.

Candidates should have passed all previous Pony Club Tests, but must have passed C+, B, Lungeing and AH. These tests will have provided a staircase of knowledge and progression to underpin the work and riding that will be observed. This will be supported by further training and practice, with different coaches and many varied horses and a wide range of reading, to give the breadth of knowledge required for this test.

Objectives
The candidates should be able to:

Show a secure, correct, balanced seat on the flat and over fences.

Improve all horses they work, including young, awkward or refusing horses.

Be able to support the practical work shown with logical theory relevant to the individual horses.

Give the examiners confidence that a horse left with the candidate would improve in his way of going.

The examiners will be looking for the following criteria:

Outside Riding
1. A balanced independent and secure position.
2. Stirrups a suitable length for riding outdoors.
3. Effective, coordinated aids, producing an appropriate response from the horse.
4. Rein aids consistent and allowing.
5. Horse 'worked in' to a logical and progressive plan.
6. Assessment of horse—specific and accurate.
7. Further work programme—individual and appropriate, for all types of horse.

Over Fences
8. Rider in balance over the horse's centre of gravity, in approach, over a fence and on landing.
9. Stirrups shortened for jumping.
10. A secure lower leg.
11. Hand allowing natural stretch over the fence.
12. Forward rhythmical pace adopted.
13. Rhythm maintained to and away from fences.
14. Horse presented to fence in a way that allows him to jump easily.
15. A smooth track between fences.
16. Ease and competence allowing the rider to appear bold whilst riding the course.
17. Proficient use of whip if necessary.
18. Accurate assessment of horse and his way of jumping.
19. Specific training plan to improve their horse's jumping.
20. Distances between related fences, doubles or grids should relate to the horse ridden, and be given in feet, yards or metres.
21. Effective logical use of fences in assessment and developing work.

Cross Country
22. Balanced position appropriate for undulating ground.
23. Secure lower leg position.
24. Effective aids, coupled with a bold attitude.
25. Rhythmical balanced pace, both in between and on approach to fences.
26. Speed suitable for the ground and training of horse.
27. Fences approached to give horse best opportunity to jump well.
28. Effective use of whip if required.
29. Clear assessment of the round ridden.

30. Understand presentation demands of specific types of fence e.g. rail and ditch combination, skinny, water, corner, bounce, etc.

Indoor Riding
Correct Classical Position
31. Secure deep seat and leg position.
32. Effective aids.
33. Consistent correct contact.
34. Horses ridden forwards in good form.
35. Accurately ridden school figures appropriate to horse's balance and level of work.
36. Logical progressive work programmes based on the Scales of Training.
37. Accurate assessment of horse's way of going.
38. Suitable specific programmes of improvement for horses ridden.
39. Knowledge of aids for all movements required.
40. Clear understanding of the preparation for all movements required.

Ability to Ride and Knowledge of When to Use:
41. Direct transitions.
42. Turn on forehand.
43. Leg yielding.
44. Travers.
45. Shoulder in.
46. Counter canter.
47. Simple change.
48. Rein back.
49. Walk pirouette.
50. Variations within the pace appropriate to horse's level of training.

Lungeing
51. Lunge line and whip handled safely.
52. Lunge line and whip handled effectively.
53. Suitable use of side reins.
54. Horse worked forwards and in balance.
55. Logical progressive work based on the Scales of Training.
56. Work in all paces as appropriate.
57. Horse worked on suitably sized circles.
58. Poles used appropriately.
59. Horse shows improvement.
60. Accurate assessment of horse's way of going.
61. Work discussed competently and confidently.
62. Appropriate ongoing training offered.

Training the Young Horse

63. Sensible knowledge of handling young stock offered.
64. Introduction to lungeing and long reining approached safely and logically.
65. Discussion of tack used appropriate for purpose.
66. Backing routine safe and practical.
67. Initial riding plan safe and suitable.
68. Appropriate ideas for widening the young horse's education.
69. Sensible use of facilities.
70. Practical time scales discussed.
71. Safety of helpers observed.

The Form of the Test

There are *four* phases to the test:

Outside Riding

During this phase, candidates will ride three or four different horses.

Having been allocated their first horse, they are allowed 5–10 minutes assessment, on the flat and over a few small fences. While doing this, they are expected to appraise the horse—his good and bad points, to be thinking what his job could be, and how he could be schooled to give a better performance and ride.

The discussion usually lasts for about 5 minutes, and the examiners expect to hear practical, common-sense answers, which would give them confidence that the candidate has the knowledge and capability of improving that particular horse or any other that he/she might be given to ride.

Candidates then change horses, and following a short assessment period will be asked to jump a show jumping round. (This is normally around 1.10 m., depending on the horses available and the ground.) The candidate will then discuss the way the horse jumped and talk about how this horse's jumping may be improved. The third horse is jumped around a short cross country course; the candidate will be assessed both over the fences and how they ride between the fences. This round may, or may not, be discussed.

Inside Riding

Candidates will ride two or three schooled horses in the indoor school.

They will be given the opportunity of assessing these horses before being asked to carry out specific movements.

One horse or more horses will be in a double bridle.

Candidates will be asked to prepare for and show movements, whilst knowing the aids to carry them out.

Depending on the standard of the horse, candidates may be asked to: ride in medium walk, working and medium trot and canter, and show some collection; show transitions and halts.

They will be required to ride some school movements such as:

- Circles, loops and serpentines of specific size
- Changes of rein
- Change of leg through trot and walk
- Counter canter loops
- Direct transitions
- Turn on the forehand
- Leg yielding
- Travers
- Shoulder-in
- Half pirouette at walk
- Rein back

Candidates will be expected to demonstrate knowledge of rules of the school. The examiners will ask the candidates to comment on the way the horses are going and performing the required movements and how the horse may be improved.

Lungeing

Candidates will lunge for about twenty minutes.

They are expected to know how to lunge for improvement, training and education (poles will be available).

Candidates will assess the horse and then lunge for improvement.

This is followed by a discussion with one assessor of how that horse worked, and what exercises were used or may be used in the future to improve his way of going.

The assessor will look to see that the horse improved whilst being lunged.

Training The Young Horse

This is a separate section, and takes the form of a discussion with the candidate's views on backing and preliminary training of a young horse, using the equipment and methods recommended by The Pony Club and explained in *Backing, Breeding and Bringing on Young Horses and Ponies*.

The Debrief

This is the last session of the day, where the candidate is given their result. Each person is debriefed individually, with the opportunity to talk to every examiner. If a candidate has not been successful this is the occasion to receive constructive ideas towards improving their level of horsemanship.

Through disappointment, it is easy to absorb only part of the conversation, and then at a later day feel they have failed due to some minor point. This is never the case, so the following points may assist the candidate to understand the reason for the lack of success:

Attend the debrief with a parent, trainer, D.C. or friend.

Take notes.

Ask questions if you are unclear on any topic.

Look at the big picture, possibly the seat was not established, which will affect every horse, rather than, 'I rode the double badly'.

Regard the debrief as an opportunity for a clear assessment on where to improve your riding.

Remember, some top riders failed the A Test the first time, so it is not the end of a promising career.

Read

The list below is by no means comprehensive. At this level candidates are encouraged to read many publications, articles and attend conventions with a wide variety of speakers.

The Manual of Horsemanship
Breeding, Backing and Bringing on Young Horses and Ponies
A Young Person's Guide to Eventing
To Be A Dressage Rider
A Young Person's Guide To Show Jumping
Look No Hands
Endurance Riding
Stablemates series: *(1) Vital Statistics*
                        (2) Body Basics
                        (3) Fit for the Bit

Suggested further reading

British Dressage Rules (FEI Definitions of Paces and movements)
The Complete Training of Horse and Rider—Alois Podhajsky
Complete Horse Riding Manual—William Micklem
Training Show Jumpers—Anthony Paalman
British Showjumping Notes on Course Designing

| **Felt Colour:** | Blue |
| **Honours:** | Purple |

WORKING FOR THE 'A' TEST 2010

This is written to explain the standard of work required to pass the 'A' Test, and to show the need for a long-term programme of preparation.

Preparation

The preparation for 'A' Test should be progressive and continuous.
The years between 'B' Test and 'A' Test must be spent in conscious preparation. Intense or 'crash' courses are rarely successful.

NOTE: You may apply to take the 'A' Test before the date of your AH Test but you will have to withdraw if you fail to pass A Test Horse and Pony Care. Candidates must have had practical experience with horses as well as ponies.

To Pass 'A' Test You Must:

- Have a genuine desire for knowledge and a need to understand the reasons behind what you do.
- Be physically fit enough to ride without strain.
- Be competent and brave enough to ride young and awkward horses.
- Have a correct riding position which has become natural, so that you will not drop back into bad habits under stress.
- Apply the aids correctly. A rider cannot expect a horse to be accurate and submissive if the aids are not clear and consistent.
- Be practical; theoretical knowledge alone is not enough. It must be accepted by the examiners that you are practised and at ease with the tasks you have been given.
- Know and understand the reasoning and logic behind the facts.
- Show the ability to get an improved performance out of all horses that you ride.
- Develop 'feel' for the way a horse is going, and know when and how to make corrections. It is even more important to be aware of when the horse is going well.
- Expand the ability to suggest plans of work for each horse as an individual, rather than generic plans that will do no harm.

A Suggested Programme of Training

On passing 'B' Test and whilst working for A Test Horse and Pony Care read the Test Sheet for 'A' Standard. Make sure you fully understand all they imply.

Work first on the areas that your 'B' Test Examiners noted.

Work continuously on your position in the saddle. Continue to ride as much as you can under instruction.

Continue with the progressive training of your own horse, using lateral work and variations within the stride to improve suppleness.

Ride as many different horses as you can and practise analysing what you think about them, using the Scales of Training as a template.

Remember that jumping is a major part of the test, so continuous practice on a variety of horses is essential to develop confidence and fluency.

Ride trained horses and ride with a double bridle to become confident in its use.

Gain competitive experience and learn to handle your 'nerves'.

Try to spend time helping in a good yard where there are plenty of horses at different levels of training, including untrained horses.

Find someone who is an experienced trainer and who uses and accepts correct Pony Club and BHS methods, and offer your services as an assistant when they are handling and training a young horse.

Be observant when looking at horses, so that you train your eye to recognise faults.

Visit horse sales and shows, with someone knowledgeable if you can, and make assessments of conformation.

Read the list of publications mentioned on the Test Sheet.

Help in your Branch as an assistant and then as a junior instructor.

Consider taking The Pony Club Coaching Certificate.

Hints about Taking the Test

Dress tidily and cleanly, wear gloves and carry a stick or whip; bring your spurs.

Arrive at the Test centre in plenty of time to walk the cross country and show jumping courses before the briefing

Keep your stirrups to a practical workmanlike length.

Don't fiddle with spurs, taking them off and putting them on again. If you are confident that you can use them correctly, it is acceptable for you to wear them. However, their misuse can be dangerous.

Look at the horse before you get on him; check the tack, look at the teeth; conformation and outlook may tell you something about the horse before you ride him.

When you first get on a strange horse and start riding, look about you and 'feel' how the horse is going. This is more relaxing and more reliable than looking at his head.

If you don't know something, say so.

If you make a mistake, admit it.

If you get in a muddle when explaining something, say so, stop, and start again.

Learn suitable distances for ground poles and related distances, which can then be adapted to suit individual horses.

Avoid the 'pat' or 'book' answer. Don't try to display all your knowledge. Instead, think seriously about the horse and then in the simplest terms possible, explain what faults there are and how you would go about overcoming them.

For example:

Q. What do you think about the way the horse is going?

A. *He is on his forehand and lazy.*

Q. How would you go about improving him?

A. *The real problem is laziness; he doesn't respond to my leg aids. This is the first thing I would correct. I would reinforce my leg aids with my stick until he became obedient. When he learns to go with more energy, I can expect more activity from his hind legs and hindquarters; he should then become a more balanced ride. It should then be possible to work to improve him.*

The 'pat' reply might have been:

A. *He needs more schooling. I would do a lot of turns, circles and transitions. Riding over undulating country might help.*

This reply is not incorrect, but it does not show real knowledge.

In the indoor riding, don't be afraid of riding the trained horse in a positive way. The trained horse is often a clever horse and knows better than most how to assess the rider's ability.

Pole Work and Jumping Distances

Set out below are distances which will suit many horses and ponies and are a sensible place to begin with a ride. However it is important to realise that all horses and ponies are individuals and that the safe distances between poles and fences will depend upon their size, type, freshness/fitness, the ability of the rider, the height of the fences and the terrain being worked over.

Horses	Metres	Feet
In Walk	1 m.	3 ft. 3 in.
In Trot	1.3–1.5 m.	4ft. 3 in.–5 ft.
In Canter	2.8 m.	9 ft.
A Placing Pole	2.8 m.	9 ft.
One non-jumping stride in trot	5.5 m.	18 ft.
Two non-jumping strides in trot	9 m.	30 ft.
One non-jumping stride canter	6.5–7.3 m.	21–24 ft.
Two non-jumping strides canter	10–11 m.	33–36 ft.
A Bounce	3.3–4.5 m.	11–15 ft.
Ponies	**Metres**	**Feet**
In Walk	0.9 m.	3 ft.
In Trot	1.1 m.	3 ft. 6 in.
In Canter	2.3 m.	7 ft. 6 in.
A Placing Pole	2.3 m.	7 ft. 6 in.
One non-jumping stride in trot	5–5.5 m.	16–18 ft.
Two non-jumping strides in trot	8.5 m.	28 ft.
One non-jumping stride canter	6.4–7.3 m.	21–24 ft.
Two non-jumping strides canter	9–10.3 m.	30–34 ft.
A Bounce	3–3.6 m.	10–12 ft.

Index

Numbers in *italics* refer to page numbers of diagrams.

Accidents (*see also* Safety precautions)
  avoiding when jumping, 52, 69
  procedures, 12
Achievement Badge Scheme, 84
Activities (*see* Forms of Instruction)
Areas (for riding), 14, 26, 27, 36
  for beginners, 26, *26*, 40
  for class lessons, 26, *26*, 27, 34, 36
  for dressage lessons, 19, 27
  for formation riding, 17, 26–27, *26*
  for jumping, 52, 58
  for road safety lessons, 20, 86
  for work on the lunge, 128
  in open country, 16
  on the road, 16
  plans of arenas, *26*, *27*
  size for double ride work, 104
Arena (*see* Area)
Assessing the ride (forming an opinion)
  in the class lesson, 36
  jumping, 56
  rider's position, 45–47, *47*
  rider's position before jumping, 59
Assistant (*see also* Forms of Instruction)
  briefing, 34
  consider using, 11
  taking beginners, 40–41
  teaching riders to jump, 57, 61, 91

Basic paces, 33
Beginners and very young riders,
  taking the ride, 41–44
  teaching to jump, 56–57
Bicycling, 117
Bits, 35, 38
Boots (footwear), 35
Bridlepaths, 84
Bridles, 35
'By rides', 100–105, *102–104*

Changing the rein, 30–31, *30*, *31*
Chief Coach/Instructor, 10, 14, *41*, 74
Circles, 29, 103–104, *104*, 106–107, *107*
  half circles, 31, *31*
Class (*see* Ride)
Class lesson, 15, 34–39
Clipping and trimming, 75
Commands (*see also* Terms)
  for halting and moving off, 32–33
  for school movements, 29–34, 101–104, 108
  for turns and changes of rein, 30–31, 102
  functions of, 29
  general advice, 29
Competitions, preparing for,
  cross-country, 94–98
  dressage tests, 87–90
  show jumping, 91–94
Concussion, 13
Condition of ponies,
  for cross-country, 98
  for hunting, 85
  for rallies, 35
  lecturing on, 78–79
Confidence,
  building for pony and rider (jumping), 52, 122
  for the beginner-rider, 40
  from the dismounted
    coach/instructor, 13
  coach/instrutors, 26
  lack of, when jumping, 60, 66

rider's, when jumping, 52, 60
Controlling the ride (*see also* Terms), 26–34, 100–108
Conventions (*see* School manners and discipline)
Cooling off (ponies or horses), 39, 57, 72, 98
Corner fences, 97
Corrections,
  during class lesson, 36
  jumping, 60–65
  rider's position, 45–47, *46*, *47*
Countryside studies, 84–85
Country ride, 16, 84
Courses, jumping,
  cross-country, 94–98
  show jumping, 91–94
  walking cross-country, 95
  walking show jumping, 91
Courteous behaviour (*see* Manners)
Cross-country,
  competition, preparing for, 94–98
  fences (*see* Jumps)
  lesson, 20

Demonstrations,
  during the class lesson, 37, 41–44
  how to give, 13
Diagonals, when trotting, 34, 43
Directive terms (*see* Terms)
Discipline, school, 33–34
Discussion (or five-minute talk), 20, 23, 78
Dismounted group lessons, 21–23, 74–78
Distance (between riders), 28, 33, 36
Distances (between jumps and trotting-poles),
  in doubles for the class lesson, 68
  in doubles for the show jumping ride, 91
  in gymnastic exercises, 116–122, *118–120*
  on gradients, 68
  trotting-poles, 117–121, *118*, *119*, *120*
  warnings, 66, 123
Ditches,
  at camps or rallies, 70
  problems at, 61
  riding cross-country, 97
Double jumps, 68, 90
Double ride, 102, 104, *102*, *104*
Dress,
  footwear, 35
  hats, 35, 52
  inspection before riding, 35–36
Dressage,
  arenas, 19, 27, *27*, 88
  lesson, 19
  tests, learning to ride, 88–90
Dressing, 101
Drill ride, 102–103

Ending the lesson,
  jumping, 57
  mounted lesson, 39
Equipment (*see* Props and Saddlery)
Exercises (*see* Physical exercises and School movements)
Expressions (*see* Terms)

Facilities (*see also* Forms of Instruction) 10–11, 14
Farming, 84
Farriers, 76–77
Faults,
  common jumping, 60–65
  rider's position, 45–47, *46*, *47*

Felt saddles, 40
Fence (*see* Jump)
Figure-of eight, 68, 106–107, 126, *107*
First aid, 12–13
Fishing, 85
Fitness of ponies, 35, 85, 98
Five-minute talk (*see* Discussion)
Footwear, 35
Forestry, 84
Formation ride, musical, 17, 108
Formation riding, 17, 26, 100–108
Forming an opinion (*see* Assessing the Ride)
Forms of Instruction (*see also* Areas, Assistant)
  Dismounted subjects,
    discussion, 23
    lecture, 23
    practical stable management, 21, 74–78, 82
    quiz, 23
    stable management tasks, 21–22
    Text book (*Manual of Horsemanship*), 10, 22
    video and DVD, 22, 80–82
  Mounted subjects,
    beginners and very young riders, 39–45
    class lesson, 15, 34–39
    country ride, 16, 84–85
    cross-country lesson, 20, 94–98
    discussion, 20
    dressage lesson, 19
    formation riding, 17, 100–118
    gymkhana games, 19
    instructional hack, 16, 84
    mock hunt, 17
    paper chase, 18
    road safety lesson, 20
    scavenger hunt, 18
    show jumping lessons, 19, 91–94

Games, 38, 40–44, *42*, *44*, 57, 58, 71, *71*
  gymkhana, 19
Girths,
  checking for tightness, 36
  inspection of, 36
'Go large', 28
Gradients,
  double jumps on, 68
  jumping on, 69
Grass-reins, fitting, 39–40
Grooming, 20, 75
Ground lines, 52, 57, 58, 68, 71
Group (*see* Ride)
Gymkhana games, 19
Gymnastic jumping, 116–122

Hack, instructional, 16, 84
Halting the ride, 32–33, *32*, *33*
Handbooks (*see* Books)
Hats, 35
Hazards,
  road safety, 86
  to be avoided when jumping, 66
Horse, Coach/Instructor's, 11, 12
  consider before teaching mounted, 12
Horsemastership, subjects
  bandaging, 75
  clipping and trimming, 75
  feeding, 20, 78
  grooming (sample lesson), 75
  mane pulling, 75
  mucking out, 75
  plaiting, 75
  saddling up, 20
  shoeing, 76–77
  tack cleaning, 20
Hunt,
  mock, 17
  scavenger, 18
Hunting, 85

'In succession', 28–29, 32, *32*
Inclining, 31, *31*, 103, *103*, 106–107, *107*
Inspection (note), 14, 35
  extra with young children, 40
Instruction,
  basics, 10–24
  forms of, 15–23
  principles of good, 12
Instructional hacks, 16, 84
Coach/Instructor
  advice for the experienced, 99–127
  position for jumping instruction, 52–55, *53*,
    54, *55*
  position in the school, 28
  qualities needed, 10
  voice, 24, 29
Introduction to the ride, 35

Jumping (*see also* Jumps), 51–72
  common problems, 60–66, *63*
  confidence, 52, 60, 61, 65, 124
  cross-country, 20, 94–98
  distances, 66, 68, 90, 117–123
  exercises, 67–72
  for more experienced coach/instructor, 116–122
  from different angles, 70, *71*
  from slow and fast speeds, 72
  from trot, 67
  gymnastic jumping, 116–122
  hazards to avoid, 66
  instruction in, 52–58
  lanes, 122
  off a circle, 67
  planning the lesson, 55
  position of ride and coach/instructor, 52–55, *53*,
    54, *55*
  rider's position, 59–66
  running out, 62, *62*
  show jumping, 19, 91–94
  slipping the reins, 63–64
  taking a lesson, 56–57
  teaching beginners (sample lesson), 57–58
  warnings, 122
Jump-off,
  timed, 94
Jumps (*see also* Jumping and Forms of Instruction)
  alongside a hedge, 53, *54*
  corner fences, 97
  construction of, 52, 53, 58, 66
  course of, cross-country, 94–98
  course of, show jumping, 91
  cross-poles, 68
  ditches, 70, 97
  doubles, 68, 91
  drop fences, 95
  good schooling fence, 58, *58*
  gymnastic, 116–122
  hogsbacks, 67
  into water, 97
  island fence and position of ride, 53, *53*
  lanes, 122
  logs, 69
  on gradients, 69, 70
  parallel, 91
  staircase, 72, 91, 122
  steeplechase, 72
  upright, 71, 91
  walls, 53–54
  with obscure landings, 96
Leading file, 28, 29, 36
Leading reins, 15, 40–41
Leaflets (*see* Books and booklets)
Leather punch, 35
Leathers (*see* Stirrup leathers)
Lectures, 22, 78–79
Lesson of the day, 11, 34, 37, 39–44
Lessons (*see* Forms of Instruction)

Loops and serpentines, 31, *31*, 106–107, *107*
Lungeing the rider, 124–128
  exercises, 126–127

'Make much of your ponies', 28
Mane pulling, 75
Manège (*see* Area)
Manners and consideration for others,
  in the countryside, 84
  in the school, 33–34
  when hunting, 85
Markers (*see* Props)
Mock hunt, 17
Mounted rides, 25–50
  controlling, 26–34
Movements (*see* School movements)
Moving off the ride, 32–33, *32*, *33*
Mucking out, 75
Music for formation rides, 108
Musical ride, 17, 108

Natural history, 84
Neckstraps,
  fitting, 39
  for beginners and young riders, 39, 59, 60, 61,
    64, 66
  for jumping, 57, 60, 62, 70
  for young ponies, 35
Notes, Coach/Instructor's, 11, 79
Numbering, 100
Numnahs, 35, 39

Open country, riding in, 16
Order of riding,
  in a class lesson, 28, 36
  in open country, 16
  on the road, 16
  senior rides, 124

Pace,
  of the leading file, 36
  of the ride, 28
  quality of, when jumping, 60
  show jumping, 91
  when hacking, 15
Paces, basic, 33
Paper chase, 18
Physical exercises,
  for specific purposes, 48–50
  in the class lesson, 37
  on the lunge. 127
  when jumping through gymnastics, 121
Plaiting, 75
Planning (*see* Preparation)
Ponies,
  condition of, 35
  conditioning, 98
  encouraging to jump well, 58
  exploitation of show jumping (note), 94
  impetuous,
    in open country, 16
    when show jumping, 59, 60
  keen, placing in class ride, 36
  kickers, 36
  lazy, when jumping, 58, 60
  pain when jumping, 66
  rewarding for good work, 28, 57, 58
  unsuitable for rallies, 35
  unsuitable for Road Safety Test, 87
  young, on the road, 16
Pony Club,
  competitions (*see* Competitions)
  syllabus of instruction, 10, 11
Position,
  Coach/Instructor's,
    in the class lesson, 24, 28
    in the jumping lesson, 52–54, *53*, *54*, *55*

  on a horse, 13, 15
rider's,
  developing, for jumping, 59–62
  encouraging rider to work on, 37
  teaching the correct, 45–47, *46*, *47*
Preparation and planning,
  before the rally, 10–11
  deciding whether to teach mounted or
    dismounted, 13
  for horsemastership lessons, 74
  for hunting, 85
  for lectures, 78–79
  for mounted lessons, 10–11, 34
  planning the jumping lesson, 55
Procedure (*see also* Forms of Instruction),
  accident, 13
  for giving a dismounted lesson, 74
  for giving a mounted class lesson, 34–39
  for taking a jumping lesson, 56–57
  for working a large ride when jumping, 55
  school manners and discipline, 33–34
Props (*see also* Forms of Instruction),
  boards, 26
  buckets with handles removed, 26, 53
  cones, 26, 40, 53
  deciding which to use, 11
  for games, 40, 41, 42
  letters, 26
  markers in the arena, 26, *26*, *27*
  markers for jumping lessons, 53, *53*
  visual aids for lectures, 79
Proving, 100

Qualities of a good Coach/Instructor, 10
Question technique, 12
Quiz, 23

Rallies, 14
  day, 14
  evening, 14
  road safety, 86–87
  working, 10, 14
Rally organisers, 14, 35, 36
Reins (*see also* Saddlery), 35
  grass, 39
  knotting the, 35
  leading, 15, 40, 41
  marking the, 40
  narrow, for small fingers, 40
  shortening, as a fault when jumping, 60
  side, when lungeing, 126–127
  slipping the, 63–64
Requirements (*see* Forms of Instruction)
Revising,
  during the mounted lesson, 37
  horsemastership, 75
Rewarding ponies for good work,
  after the jump, 58
  kind word and pat, 57
  'make much of your ponies', 28
  relief from carrying weight, 57
Ride, going for a,
  country or instructional hack, 15–16, 84
Ride (class or group)
  beginners and very young, 39–45
  controlling the, 26–34
  dismounted, taking the, 73–82
  mounted, procedures for taking the, 34–39
  preparation for taking the, 10
  working-in the, 36
Rider's position (*see* Position)
Road safety, 16, 20, 86–87
Running out, 62, *62*

Saddle room, 21
Saddlery or tack (*see also* Neckstraps, Reins,
  Stirrup leathers)

bits, 35
bridles, 21, 35
cleaning, 21, 75
condition of, 35
felt saddles, 40
girths, 35, 36
grass-reins, 39
inspection of, 14 (note), 35, 40
leading reins, 16, 40, 41
numnahs, 35, 39
saddles, 20, 35
safety stirrups, 40
side reins, when lungeing, 125–126
stirrup bars, 40
stirrups. 35, 40, 48
Saddles, 20, 35
felt, 40
Saddling up, 20
Safety precautions (*see also* Accidents)
    closing gates, 40
    discretion with physical exercises, 49
    distance between riders, 28
    extra checks of young riders' saddlery, 40
    first aid, 12–13
    fluorescent strips when on the road, 15
    footwear, 35
    hats, 35
    inspection of equipment, 35–36
    neckstraps, 39
    special considerations with junior rides, 40
    when jumping, 52, 123
    with nervous ponies (physical exercises), 48
Sample lessons (*see also* Forms of Instruction)
    first jumping lesson, 57
    for beginners and young riders, 41–45
    grooming, 75
    moving off and stopping, 41
    other subjects, using lesson
        plan for grooming, 75
    rising trot, 43
    shoeing, 76–77
    teaching riders to jump, 57–58
    teaching the correct
        position, 45–47, 46, 47
    transition to canter, 43–44
    turns and circles, 41–42
Scavenger hunt, 18
School (*see also* Areas), 26, 101
School manners and discipline, 33–34
School movements,
    changes of rein, 30–31, 30, 31
    circles, 29, 103–104, 104, 106–107, 107
    half circles, 31, 31
    half figures-of-eight, 106–107, 107
    halting the ride, 32, 32, 33, 33
    inclining, 31, 31, 103, 103, 106–107, 107
    loops and serpentines, 31, 31, 106–107, 107
    moving off the ride, 32–33, 32, 33
    turns across the school, 30, 30
Seat (*see* Position)
Seat bones, 50, 124
Serpentines and loops, 31, 31, 106–107, 107
Shooting, 84
Show jumping,
    course for, 91
    lesson, 19, 90–94
    preparing for competition, 91–94, 92
Single file, 28–31, 30, 31
'Sit at ease', 28, 34
Slipping the reins, 63–64
Speed of leading file, 28
Stable management (*see* Horsemastership)
Stage (or standard) of rides,
    consider, in preparation, 10
Steeplechase fence, 72
Stirrup bars, 40
Stirrup leathers (*see also* Saddlery),

adjusting, 36, 46
altering (a game), 38
inspecting, 35
lengths for beginners, 40
shortening for jumping, 56, 59
too long for jumping, 65
Stirrups,
    exercises without, 48, 55, 125
    inspection of, 35
    safety, 40
Syllabus of Instruction for the Pony Club, 10, 11

Tack (*see* Saddlery)
Tack room (*see* Saddle room)
Tantivies, 98
Task,
    stable management, 20
    system of working senior rides, 123
Teaching (*see* Instruction)
Terms (directive). *See also* Commands and
    Controlling
    the ride, 28–34, 100–105
    bicycling, 106
    'by rides' (*see* By rides')
    changing the rein, 30, 31, 30, 31
    direction, 28
    distance, 28
    dividing into rides, 100
    double ride (*see* Double ride)
    dressing, 101
    'go large', 28
    in single file (*see* Single file)
    in succession, 28, 29, 32, 32,
    leading file, 28, 29, 36
    left rein, 28
    'make much of your ponies', 28
    numbering, 100
    pace, 28, 33, 36
    proving, 100
    rear file, 28
    right rein, 28
    'sit at ease', 28
    speed, 28
    tracks, 28
    tricycling, 105–107, 106, 107
    'walk on a loose/long rein', 28, 34, 64, 94
    'whole ride', 29, 100
Tracks, 28, 33, 62
    left/right, 28
    outer/inner, 28
Tricycling, 105–107, 107
Trotting-poles, 116–122 118, 119, 120
Turns across the school, 30, 30

Unsuitable ponies,
    for rallies, 35
    for road safety, 87

Video and DVD, 22, 80–82
Visual aid for lectures, 79
Voice, use of the, 24

Walking the course (*see* Courses)
'Walk on a long/loose rein', 28, 34, 64, 94
Warming down (ponies or horses), 11, 39, 57, 72,
    94, 98
Whips, 34, 39, 61, 63
'Whole ride', 28–29, 32, 33, 100, 104
Words of command (*see also* Terms and
    Expressions), 29
Working-in the ride, 36
Working rallies (*see* Rallies)

Young riders, teaching, 34–44